BRAND SENSE

BRAND SENSE

SENSORY SECRETS BEHIND THE STUFF WE BUY

2nd edition

MARTIN LINDSTROM

LONDON PHILADELPHIA NEW DELHI

Publisher's note

Every possible effort has been made to ensure that the information contained in this book is accurate at the time of going to press, and the publishers and authors cannot accept responsibility for any errors or omissions, however caused. No responsibility for loss or damage occasioned to any person acting, or refraining from action, as a result of the material in this publication can be accepted by the editor, the publisher or any of the authors.

First published in the United States in 2005 by Free Press, a division of Simon & Schuster, Inc., 1230 Avenue of the Americas, New York, NY 10020, USA.
Trade paperback edition, 2010

First published in Great Britain in 2005 by Kogan Page Limited
This edition, 2010
Reprinted 2010, 2012

Kogan Page Limited
120 Pentonville Road
London N1 9JN
United Kingdom
www.koganpage.com

Text designed by Paul Dippolito
All illustrations were created by Martin Lindstrom

British Library Cataloguing in Publication Data

A CIP record for this book is available from the British Library.

ISBN 978 0 7494 6057 0

Printed and bound in India by Replika Press Pvt. Ltd.

For Dorit, Tore, Vibeke, and Allan
You are the words in my life

Tell me and I'll forget,
Show me and I might remember,
Involve me and I'll understand.

—BENJAMIN FRANKLIN

Contents

Foreword

Philip Kotler

MARKETING ISN'T WORKING TODAY. New products are failing at a disastrous rate. Most advertising campaigns do not register anything distinctive in the customer's mind. Most products come across as interchangeable commodities rather than powerful brands.

Yes, there are still powerful brands—Coca Cola, Harley-Davidson, Apple Computer, Singapore Airlines, BMW. They have learned how to make their brand live in the customers' minds. The brand, of course, must at least deliver a distinctive benefit. No amount of dressing up will make up for this lack. All of the aforementioned brands deliver a distinctive benefit.

But distinctive brands require something more. They have to be powered up to deliver a full sensory and emotional experience. It is not enough to present a product or service visually in an ad. It pays to attach a sound, such as music or powerful words and symbols. The combination of visual and audio stimuli delivers a 2 + 2 = 5 impact. It further pays to trigger other sensory channels—taste, touch, smell—to enhance the total impact. This is Martin Lindstrom's basic message, and he illustrates it beautifully through numerous cases with compelling arguments.

Most companies take the easy way out to market their brands. They buy a lot of expensive advertising and make clichéd claims. The companies in Martin's book are much more creative. One of the main reasons to read this book is that it contains a treasury of ideas for bringing new life to brands.

CHAPTER 1

Start Making Sense

IN THE WEEKS AND MONTHS FOLLOWING publication of *Buyology: Truth and Lies About Why We Buy*, I was invited to appear frequently on America's most popular morning program, the *Today* show. The topics we covered were various—shopping addictions, whether sex in advertising sells, subliminal advertising, and so on. During a recent appearance, I carried out a focus group with a selection of tweens, ages eight through twelve. My goal? To measure the degree to which sensory branding—that is to say, the use of fragrances, sounds, and even textures to enhance the appeal of products—affected these kids. It was like emceeing a strange new game show called "Name That Sense."

First I played a handful of well-known songs associated with various well-known companies and TV shows. Most of the children were able to name them immediately, among them Disney, Apple Computer, and the signature theme music from Spongebob Squarepants and NBC. Now it was time for the smell test. The first fragrance that floated out was (and will always be) one of the most evocative aromas in the world.

"Oh, I know that smell," one said.

"Every kid knows that smell," another broke in.

"Okay," I said. "On the count of three, you're going to tell me what the brand is. Ready? One . . . two . . . three—"

They all got it: Play-Doh! The next two fragrances? Crayola crayons and Johnson's Baby Powder. The children identified those, too. Next, we graduated to a brand "collage board," where only parts or fragments of companies' logos or symbols were visible. Still, the kids were able to identify most if not all of the brands, from Kellogg's to Pepsi-Cola to MTV to Nike. Some, to my surprise, were even able to recognize the logos of Gucci and Tiffany's.

After scanning a handful of logos, I brought out a bunch of products from high-end designers, popular department stores, and even some generic clothing I'd picked up from street vendors.

Now, blue jeans are a not uncomplicated item for most fashion- and brand-obsessed middle-schoolers. One of the girls—Olivia—cradled a pair of jeans in her lap.

"These are from Abercrombie!" she announced happily.

As offhandedly as I could, I asked, "So how do you know those jeans are *really* from that store, and not fake?"

"Because of their *smell*," Olivia replied. She then proceeded to inhale the sweet (some might say sickly sweet) fragrance of the Abercrombie & Fitch jeans she was holding.

What Olivia was holding looked like any other pair of blue jeans. They could have come from Target. They could have come from Macy's. They could have come from a factory outlet anywhere in America. But this middle-school student had identified those jeans without blinking for one reason only: their unmistakable aroma.

As strange and intriguing as Olivia's brand preference might sound, my appearance on the *Today* show couldn't help but remind me of the first worldwide sensory branding research project I ever carried out, which concluded in 2005. It was a five-year mission involving hundreds of researchers and thousands of consumers across four continents. Our goal was to understand the rationale behind behavior like Olivia's—and provide a road map for consumers to understand why they were drawn to a product, whether it was an iPod, a jar of Nescafé coffee, or even a simple breakfast cereal.

Olivia, after all, was a living, breathing example of what marketers aspire to when they create a brand. I've long wondered: What is it that makes a child (or for that matter, an adult) fall head over heels for a brand like Apple or Kellogg's? What components of the brand form such a magical, magnetic, long-lasting connection? Does an obsessive belief in a brand ever wilt into disappointment or even boredom?

That is why in 2005's Project Brand Sense, my team and I went out and asked all kinds of questions of people who have strong affinities for various brands—in some cases, you might even call them love affairs. They willingly, and generously, shared their passions and insights—invaluable information that led me to conclude that if products and advertising want to survive another century, they'll need to change direction entirely. Yet another ad plastered on a billboard in Times Square simply won't do the trick. An entirely new—and sensory—vision, one that appeals to our emotions, is what's required.

I realized then, as I do now, that a brand *has* to transform itself into a sensory experience that goes far beyond what we see. I also realized that more than anyone on the planet, children seem to bond most profoundly with brands that are truly sensory—that involve sound, touch, smell, and feel. This may not come as a shock when you consider that a typical child's senses are approximately 200 percent more potent than an adult's. In fact, when a new mother first cradles an infant, she probably has no idea that a newborn's sense of smell is more than 300 percent greater than her own. Call it nature's ingenious way of securing a permanent bond between mother and child.

Let me give you another amazing example of the power of sensory branding. Royal Mail is the national postal service of the United Kingdom. As many people know, postal administrations all over the world are suffering massive declines in revenue. Very few people are sending mail nowadays—packages, sure, but not those white things known as envelopes with something called a stamp placed on its upper right-hand corner. When you think about it, when was the last time you received a handwritten letter in your mailbox? The world far prefers the convenience of email, Facebook, and Twitter.

In order to breathe new life into its declining direct mail figures, Royal Mail launched a campaign known as "Touching Bands." Its aim was twofold: to reconnect with consumers who'd drifted away from what was now termed somewhat dismissively "snail mail," and to demonstrate direct mail's pivotal role in the digital age as a natural partner to new media. The UK-based Brand Sense Agency was tapped to help them explore how we can use our five senses to enhance our affinity to a brand—in this case Royal Mail. The experiment was dubbed "Sensational Mail." The results were, well, sensational.

The first piece of "Sensational" Royal Mail sent out was a personalized letter inscribed on a slab of chocolate—you read that right. Who can resist chocolate—the smooth touch, the smell that makes us salivate, the cracking sound as you break the bar in two, and last but not least, the taste?

Praised as being innovative and eye-catching, the overall response to our Royal Mail chocolate mailing defied all expectations. Three quarters of all its recipients felt it demonstrated how direct mail could engage all five senses, but they also took some action as a result of our mailing experiment, action, I should emphasize, that went over and beyond eating the chocolate letter. Quite simply, they started sending out letters again!

But we wanted to confirm our findings scientifically as well for media planners and advertisers. Using neuroscience and the most advanced brain-scanning technique available today—the fMRI—global research institute Millward Brown studied the brains of twenty men and women in the UK to find out whether the "Royal Mail experiment" had created true emotional engagement, that is to say, a potent emotional response, in consumers. They wanted to see if volunteers' brains responded at all differently to material via direct mail than they did to comparable information shown them on a computer screen. For any brand, ad, or entreaty to work (and remain memorable), it has to make its way somehow into the overstuffed workspace that is the human brain. As you might imagine, our brains are adept at filtering out irrelevant information. Emotion gets our attention through our senses—which then influence our decision-making processes. Brands that create an emotional connection to consumers are much stronger than those that don't—it's as simple (and complicated) as that.

Millward Brown's scientific research study confirmed that direct mail—namely, those chocolate-laden entreaties—was far more "real" to the brain, and had a definite "place" in consumers' perceptions. Moreover, direct mail was easier for the volunteers' brains to process, more likely than not to generate emotion, and also able to promote more fluent decision making. In short, the Royal Mail experiment proved conclusively that direct mail was able to penetrate the overcrowded closet that is our mental workspace—a spectacular feat, considering that the majority of us live in an increasingly digital environment.

Another aspect of the new branding I gleaned from my experiences with Olivia and Royal Mail is that a brand should attempt to create a following akin to the obsessive adoration a sports fan feels or even, in some respects, the faith of a religious congregation.

Without taking comparisons to religion too far, we can see the relevance of spirituality for certain aspects of sensory branding. The most memorable, savored brands of the future will be those that not only anchor themselves in tradition, but also adopt religious characteristics as they simultaneously make full, integrated use of sensory branding—period. Each fully integrated brand will boast its own identity, one that's expressed in its every message, shape, symbol, ritual, and tradition—just as sports teams and religion do.

Evoking something resembling religious zeal, however, is only one objective of the next generation of products and advertising. In order to survive, brands will have to incorporate a brand "platform" (meaning a set of associations a consumer makes with a product, or company) that fully unites the five senses. Witness Abercrombie! We live in a landscape where consumers desperately need something to believe in. Ironic though it may sound, as religions struggle to find new constituents, consumers in contrast are desperately seeking something else. Sadly (some might say), more than ever that "something else" is, well, brands—a phenomenon you would appreciate even more if you visited China, where the power of "brand religion" often seems even stronger than its thousand-year-old faith-based counterparts.

The foundation of this book is a direct result of an extensive research project that sought to investigate the role each of our five senses plays in creating a passionate love affair between a consumer and a brand. Our study also sought to determine to what extent a religious factor—faith, belief, belonging, and community—might serve to guide the future of branding. At first glance, religion and brands might seem almost insultingly far apart. But are they really? Visit any church and even before you enter the building, the first thing you'll notice is a full-frontal sensory assault, whether it's the noontime bells pealing across Zurich, Switzerland, or the sounds of prayer overwhelming Istanbul. Inside a church, your senses will continue to be stirred and awakened, whether it's from the unmistakable fragrance of incense in the air, or the musty odor of the pews. No matter where you live, or what faith you practice, religion sends a series of clear, unmistakable signals via your senses—even if you never glimpse a cross, an altar, a stained glass window, or a yarmulke. Our oldest religions have been around for roughly 3,500 years. Our oldest brands? One hundred and fifty years. That is why I believe that it may be time for brands to borrow respectfully from religion—and learn a few crucial lessons about belief and loyalty.

Moreover, we decided that our Brand Sense study would have relevance only if conducted globally. Our multicultural research team involved people drawn from twenty-four countries, and speaking eighteen languages. Additionally, our global research study had another objective. We wanted to identify growing trends, and explore the evolution of local brands to help us create a solid foundation for the implementation of our fully integrated brand theory, in order for it to adapt to any market regardless of cultural differences and preferences.

I decided to team up with Millward Brown, whose extensive brand knowledge made them an obvious partner for a project of this caliber. The idea—which we dubbed "Brand Sense"—took seed in 1999 and eventually developed into a brand research project that involved some six hundred researchers across the globe.

Let me be frank—no one had ever carried out research on sensory perception and religious comparisons to branding before, and we tried our best to remain sensitive to their differences in character, profundity, and ultimate truth. My publisher was seriously concerned, and not unreasonably, either, as I began this book. I went so far as to conduct a series of sessions across the United States to test out my theories in front of live audiences. In particular, I recall one speaking engagement in Washington, D.C., where I showed a photograph of the pope on one side of the screen, and Ronald McDonald on the other. Being a native of Denmark, where traditional faith barely exists, I learned quickly (extremely quickly) that many people elsewhere are highly sensitive about the topic of religion. A classic live-and-learn experience.

Project Brand Sense is therefore (dare I say it?) a pioneering study. We conducted focus groups in thirteen countries, selecting each country on the basis of its market size, brand representation, general product innovations, religious representation, state of brand maturity, not to mention the country's sensory history. We swiftly learned that even though a brand is supposedly global, the way local cultures perceive it can be extremely varied.

The Brand Sense study therefore is a composite of distinct and different markets. For instance, we selected Japan, India, and Thailand because all three countries have a long-standing history of integrating five senses within their culture and traditions. Some of Japan's most innovative brands often make use of the five senses. Now, if you're ever in a hurry, don't expect a grab-and-go experience if you're visiting a Japanese retail store. But there's a fantastic upside. Your transaction may not be speedy, but you'll get to witness a truly astonishing, sometimes half-hour-long, wrapping ritual, and your purchase will typically end up resembling an exquisitely beribboned work of art. Japan, after all, is the nation where brands like Marlboro found out that placing a little dotted line in the plastic foil enveloping its iconic cigarette packs transformed sales from sluggish to impressive. Why, you might ask? Because the Japanese hate the sensation of unwrapping a box of cigarettes where the foil tears up or shreds all over the box. By installing a minuscule touch such as a simple dotted line, consumers could easily open the pack without desecrating the pack's graphics. That simple tweak positively transformed Marlboro's sales in a matter of weeks.

The rich design heritage of the Scandinavian countries has made visual identity essential to their communication. It's one region in the world where a designer's hand is evident everywhere—from condoms for women to pill bottle openers. The United States and Britain, with their huge market size and diverse media, present the biggest challenge in building and maintaining brands. We also included countries like Chile, Mexico, Poland, and Spain because of their strong religious and devotional traditions, or because of their long-standing history with music and food.

But no matter where you live, think about it: Our values, our feelings, our emotions, our memories—they're all stored in our brains. Compare this human filing system to an old-fashioned video recorder, which records on two separate tracks, one for image, one for sound. Human beings have at least five tracks—image, sound, smell, taste, and touch. These tracks contain more data than one can imagine and they have direct, immediate bearing on our emotional life. They can fast-forward or rewind at will, even linger on a precise spot. The more tracks on which you or I can record an experience, the better we remember it.

For this reason, I believe that over the next decade we'll witness seismic shifts in the way we as consumers perceive brands. A comparison that springs to mind is the transition from black-and-white to color television with mono sound, to high-definition fifty-two-inch Magnolia home theaters with all the bells and whistles.

So fasten your seat belts. You're about to embark on a sensory journey—which I hope will ensure that you'll never again see (or smell) a brand quite the same way again.

CHAPTER 2

Maybe I'm Doing It Right?

FACT: MOST BRANDING CAMPAIGNS are in trouble. Why? Because the cost of reaching consumers in a frenetic, overstimulating, ADHD-like world is increasing *fast*. Household television viewing hours are increasingly the domain of children. In America, the average child is exposed to more than 40,000 television commercials a year—and a typical adult is exposed to more than 52,000.[1] To put it another way, the average sixty-five-year-old American has viewed more than two million commercials—which adds up to six full years of watching eight hours a day, seven days a week![2]

That's a lot of screen time.

Given these TV-viewing statistics, it probably comes as no surprise that U.S. television advertising spending in 2008 was $69.8 billion. Every year, several thousand new brands appear on store shelves that need to be introduced to consumers. Have you ever shaken hands with an individual whose clammy, soggy handshake reminded you of a limp fish? In two seconds, you had that person pegged as, well, spineless or lacking in character somehow. Brands have an equal amount of time—approximately two seconds—to make an instantaneous impression on us. Not surprisingly, most of them underwhelm us and a year later, are no longer to be found on the supermarket shelves.

Advertising may not work the way it's supposed to, but it's not going anywhere soon. Maybe the way marketers communicate their messages has to be reevaluated or, rather, better aligned with the *rat-a-tat* tempo of today's world. I know this much: Something altogether revolutionary is required to break our present-day advertising impasse. Razor-sharp picture quality won't cut it; neither will snazzier graphics. What about increasingly creative ideas set to digital sound? That's not the answer either. No matter what we do, advertising remains an instantly forgettable flash in the day-to-day life of a consumer—and we're only at the beginning. In Japan, where the average consumer watches the equivalent of eight years of TV commercials over his or her lifetime (a reminder: that's two years more than in the United States), I can tell you that the future picture isn't pretty.

But . . . what if marketers threw all that out, and instead tried to inject as many senses as possible within their messages? Would *that* work? Just think about how you generally make decisions. Imagine you're considering hiring a new employee. The first thing you'd do is scan his or her resume, and follow up with an introductory chat on the phone. If your potential employee happened to live, say, in another country, you might even arrange a videoconference call. Yet you would probably never agree to hire someone unless you met him or her in person—am I right? Why? What possible advantage could you gain by meeting a potential employee face to face? He or she wouldn't speak defiantly, wouldn't gesture any differently and would know no more or no less than what he or she had already communicated. Fact is, nothing would change—so why is a face-to-face meeting so important?

Behavioral psychologists today estimate that up to 80 percent of all the impressions we form when communicating with other people are nonverbal. That is to say, they're sensory. *That's* why you need to meet a prospective employee before you hire him or her.

So back to branding: Why then have businesses and marketers eliminated a full 80 percent of what they could communicate when they build brands? Skeptics rightly point out that smell and television are a physical impossibility. I would respond that even though a brand is unable to impart a fragrance via a forty-two-inch LCD, there's very little stopping an aroma from being fully integrated *within* a brand.

Something to Sniff At . . .

You take a whiff of the milk in the refrigerator before taking a gulp. Is there the faintest hint of sourness? If so, it'll probably go straight down the drain. Our sense of smell keeps us safe by helping us choose fresh (and avoid rotten) food. Each piece of fruit and cut of meat that lands in our shopping carts has passed the sniff and feel test. Instinctively we check for suspicious tears in the packaging and wait, subconsciously, for the breathless *ahhhh* of the seal when we snap open a soda or a can of peanuts. Recently, when I was visiting India, I bought some bottled water. I unscrewed the top, waiting for the familiar *click* sound that reassured me I was about to drink something fresh. When no sound came, I was frankly disconcerted, as if I'd be poisoned if I drank the thing.

Our senses are far more attuned to possible danger than to the expectation of sensory delight. And over the past century the advertising world has indulged and catered to our sense of sight, ensuring optimal visual satisfaction. That gorgeous new iPhone. That stunning dress in the window of Zara. That shapely new bottle of designer perfume. At the same time, it's as though we've forgotten that every man, woman, and child on the planet is endowed with not just two, but five senses. I remember once when my dad told me about a journey he'd taken when he was very young with his own father to buy coffee. The moment the two of them set foot in the store, they could smell the enticing aroma of freshly ground coffee as the powdery beans streamed into a paper bag. Accompanying the fragrance was the sound the machine made as it pulverized the beans. Can the smell of a just-brewed pot of coffee even compare to that multisensory experience?

Half a century later, it's a different story. Enter Walmart or any contemporary supermarket. Go to the coffee aisle and you'll find shelves of vacuum-sealed bricks of ground and whole coffee beans, packaged to fit the thousands of trucks that deliver coffee and other products daily. Where's the aroma? There is none. The machine sound? With the exception of Starbucks, there is none (though Starbucks has its own problems, which we'll get into later). Sure, there may be a primitive image on the package of a Colombian farm worker hard at work grinding beans, but it's not the same. That said, packaging is now a major selling point for advertisers and marketers, as the appearance of a product still has a potent influence in attracting consumer attention. (If it works, that is. On a flight I once took from New York to L.A., I bought a pair of earphones and proceeded to extract the earphones from their plastic "clamshell" sealing. Or rather, I should say, *tried*. Half an hour later, I was still trying to wrench off the plastic, even using my plastic serrated dinner knife. Even my seatmate joined in—until finally, three rows of passengers were gallantly attempting to extract my earphones. Finally, with about fifteen minutes left in the flight, someone managed to tear open the packaging, but by then it was too late.)

If a product carries a sound, touch, taste, and smell component, you'd probably be right in assuming this is merely a happy coincidence. On the other hand, you might rightly wonder why these four senses have been neglected for so long. Let's do an experiment. Imagine you have two bottles of Heinz ketchup in your kitchen. One is plastic, the other glass. Having visited hundreds (if not thousands) of kitchens across the world, my educated guess is that if you had two bottles, the glass one would be inside your fridge, while the plastic one would reside unopened in your cupboard. Why? Because most if not all of us perceive the glass ketchup bottle as being not only authentic but *sensory*. That said, a glass bottle of ketchup is almost comically impractical. You unscrew the top, tip it over onto your cheeseburger . . . and nothing comes out. Five minutes later, it's still the same, unless you've begun violently pounding the back of the bottle.

When Heinz invented ketchup in 1869, all bottles were glass. As time went by, the unfunctional reality of extracting ketchup from a glass bottle became evident to everybody. So roughly 25 years ago, Heinz did something ingenious. The company released a print campaign stating, "Heinz ketchup exits the iconic glass bottle at .028 miles an hour." At first, if you're anything like me, you want to laugh, maybe even mutter, "So? What does that have to do with anything, particularly ketchup?" The answer: Heinz isn't claiming that their ketchup is of the highest caliber in the world. Instead, they're appealing to our ancient human instinct that equates "slow" with "high quality" (just as flimsy and fast often connotes crummy or half-hearted handiwork). Our brains connect the dots and in less than a second, we decide that the long wait Heinz ketchup demands is worth it—because ultimately, we're getting the best possible product. Our suffering hasn't been in vain after all! Yet has Heinz ever come right out and said this? Not once. (Lest we forget, the company also rolled out a memorable TV ad back in the 1970s using Carly Simon's song "Anticipation," as a consumer waited . . . and waited . . . for that damn ketchup to come out of the bottle.) Today, in 2010, you'll see Heinz's glass ketchup bottles in every convenience store and supermarket across America. They're more expensive, more breakable, heavier, the ketchup still pours only with great difficulty—yet 80 percent of the respondents in our Brand Sense study preferred the glass bottle over the plastic one. When asked why, they shrugged their shoulders. They had no idea—but their subconscious did.

The fact is that we experience practically our entire understanding of the world via our senses. They're our link to memory. They tap into our emotions, past and present. A bright, fresh, glorious spring day has a particularly bracing smell. Naturally, manufacturers try to bottle this distillation of seasonal euphoria and renewal. Marketers then use our emotional connection to spring to sell us their dishwashing liquids, toilet cleaners, shampoos, soaps, window cleaners, you name it.

Incorporating our five senses has worked spectacularly well in emotionally connecting people to the rituals of faith. Think about it: the votive candles flicker; the incense burns and smokes; the choir bursts forth into rousing songs of devotion. There's pageantry, elaborate costumes, communion, foods for special occasions. Even the sixth sense is given a special place in the pantheon of world religions.

I was recently strolling down a Tokyo street when I brushed past a woman who was wearing a perfume that smelled familiar. Whoosh—a treasure box of memories and emotions immediately began flooding my consciousness. That fragrance took me back fifteen years to my high school days when I had a close friend who wore the precise same scent. For a brief moment Tokyo faded away as I stood there, frozen back in Denmark (figuratively *and* literally, given how frigid it is there), overcome by the familiar fragrance, and the happy, sad, fearful, confusing memories of adolescence.

Our memory libraries begin accumulating material from the second we're born. Fluid and flexible, that library is constantly open to redefinition and reinterpretation. When Russian physiologist Ivan Pavlov rolled out his famous experiment in 1899, he proved to the world that a dog can be taught to anticipate food by the sound of a bell. And that reflexive behavior extends to humans.

Think about your bedside alarm. As it shrills its wake-up call in the morning, you may have come to dread the noise it makes. If, for some reason, you heard the same sound in the middle of the day, it wouldn't be remotely surprising to experience that same *oh-no* sense of queasy foreboding.

From the moment we wake up to the moment we go to sleep, moods, feelings, and even the products in our lives are continuously imprinted on our five-track sensory recorder. We've grown accustomed to the metallic sound of our spoon stirring sugar in our coffee cups, the glassy *ding* of an email arriving on our computers, the shiver of our BlackBerries vibrating, the characteristic ditty AT&T plays when we're calling a friend long-distance. We're even familiar with, and emotionally transported by, the beeping sound at McDonald's, or the four o'clock closing bell that sounds at the New York Stock Exchange. Studies have shown that brands that incorporate sound onto the home pages of their websites are 76 percent more likely to obtain repeat Internet traffic—and that brands with music that "fit" their brand identity are 96 percent likelier to prompt memory recall.[3] Yet funnily enough, few brands have decided to take advantage of, or "own" a specific sound. Why is that?

Every day we may be overwhelmed by mass communication, including advertising messages, but mostly it appeals only to two of the five available tracks: eyes and ears, the visual and the auditory. We're so accustomed to this two-barreled approach we don't give it a second thought. Therein lies the paradox. As human beings, we're by far at our most receptive when we're operating on all five tracks (our five senses), yet very few advertising campaigns bother to use more than sight and sound to convey their messages.

Remember when you bought your first new car? It had a definite—and intoxicating—new-car smell. (I'll bet if you close your eyes, you can smell it now.) Many people cite that leathery aroma as being among the most gratifying moments of purchasing a new auto. As much as the shiny body, the pristine seats, and the whitewall tires, that smell announces and exudes never-before-driven *newness*.

I hate to disappoint you, but there's no such thing as a new-car smell—at least an organic one. It, the "New Car" fragrance, can be found packed in aerosol-filled canisters on the factory floor. As the car leaves the production line, an autoworker spritzes the fragrance throughout the interior. The smell generally lasts about six weeks before it's overtaken by the rough and tumble of dirty running shoes, old magazines, dry cleaning, and the stained empty coffee cup you gulped from on your way to work.

The "New Car" fragrance is a marketing ploy that taps directly and successfully into fantasy. Recently, in fact, Mitsubishi's ad agency placed a fragrance ad in two major newspapers that simulated that leathery "new car" smell. The result: the company's Lancer Evo X sold out in two weeks and the car company's sales increased by 16 percent, even during a recession.[4]

Ironically, neither the speedometer nor your efforts at fastidiousness can define when your car is no longer "new"—it's the slowly ebbing new-car smell that creates the demarcation between a new and a no-longer-quite-as-new everyday item. Of course, you can always prolong that sense of newness (and fantasy) by paying a visit to your local car accessory store and buying a can of the new-car smell yourself!

A few years ago, a friend of mine had a strange encounter while cruising around in his new car. His young daughter was in the back seat. My friend isn't the most skillful driver in the world and at one point he swerved sharply, ultimately getting into a minor accident.

His daughter's face turned green and she got sick all over the back seat. That, sadly, was the day his car lost its fabled New Car Smell. And, as he later told me, that was also the day he lost his "new car."

As a species, we're surprisingly oblivious to the way our senses interact with our day-to-day experiences. Across from a popular beach near where I live is a row of stores selling all manner of summertime equipment: umbrellas, sarongs, boogie boards, sun creams, sodas, and so on. On a cold winter's day, when a rough southerly wind was blowing, a friend who needed to buy a last-minute birthday present popped into one of these stores to scan the jewelry section. Without knowing why, she suddenly found herself browsing the swimsuit rack. Taken aback by her own behavior, she slowly became aware that the surrounding air seemed suffused with summer even though swimming season was a good five months away. Later, joking around with the sales staff, she asked them to reveal their unseasonable secrets. A clerk led her to a corner of the store, and pointed to a machine that was pumping out a subtle but discernible smell of coconuts. (In the end, she didn't buy the swimsuit, but a week later she booked a trip to Fiji.)

You can find that same power of suggestion everywhere. In Hong Kong to welcome several incoming flights of Germans, management once played accordion music throughout the entire airport. I, and just about everybody else, felt as though I'd somehow ended up in Berlin. Kellogg's, the breakfast cereal experts, believes we are equally affected by the textures we consume as by the flavor of the food. Rice Krispies (known in parts of the world as Rice Bubbles) that fail to snap, crackle, and pop are dismissed by most consumers as stale, even though the taste is no different, and the cereal may in fact still be perfectly good. So it's hardly surprising that Kellogg's considers the crunchiness of the grain as having *everything* to do with the triumph of its brand, which is why their TV ads emphasize the *crunch* we hear and feel in our mouths.

Kellogg's has spent years exploring the linkage between crunch and taste. The company hired a Danish laboratory that specializes in creating the precise crunchy *sound* of a breakfast cereal. Not surprisingly, Kellogg's wanted to patent, trademark, and "own" the crunch, just as they own their recipe and logo. The laboratory created a highly distinctive crunch especially designed for Kellogg's, with one critical distinction: The particular sound and feel of the crunch was identifiably, unmistakably Kellogg's, and anyone who happened to select a bowl of cornflakes at a breakfast buffet would be able to recognize those anonymous flakes as Kellogg's at the first bite.

The day Kellogg's introduced their one-of-a-kind crunch to the market, their brand began to go through the roof. Why? Because they'd expanded the perception of their brand to incorporate four senses (including touch) rather than merely sight and sound.

Brands that appeal to as many senses as possible make, well, sense. According to University of Michigan authors Ryan S. Elder and Aradhna Krishna, "Because taste is generated from multiple senses—smell, texture, sight and sound—ads mentioning these senses will have a significant impact on taste over ads mentioning taste alone." In one experiment the two researchers carried out, volunteers were exposed to one of two advertisements for chewing gum. One was a gum whose tagline read, "Stimulate your senses" while the other tagline, "Long-lasting flavor," appealed simply to the taste buds. According to Mr. Elder, "The multiple-sense ad led to more positive sensory thoughts, which then led to higher taste perception than the single-sense ad. The difference in thoughts was shown to drive the differences in taste."[5]

Imagine walking past a bakery where you can smell the heat coming off the bread. It doesn't often happen. Visitors to Northern European supermarkets will notice that freshly baked bread is prominently displayed at the entryways to the stores. Although there's no bakery anywhere nearby, if they look up carefully at the ceiling they'll spot a series of vents specifically designed to disperse baking aromas. Typically sales are high—not only of baked goods, but across all product lines.

In Hong Kong, to cater to the growing demand for hygiene, one market I know of has installed the bakery in the main entrance. Large plate-glass windows allow customers a peek at where the bread and pastries are baked and produced. Customers can watch every move the baker makes, while the smell is deliberately, carefully canalized to satisfy the sensory buttons the store wants to push in order to create consumer hunger. Needless to say, even during the 2009 recession the store did booming business.

Bloomingdale's does the same thing by pumping the smell of Johnson's Baby Powder into their stores. Sony and Samsung both pump in proprietary fragrances which make their customers feel unaccountably serene. Once, in a do-it-yourself store in Germany, customers began smelling—could it be?—the aroma of freshly cut grass. Later, when consumers were queried about their impressions of the place, the positive response had risen by nearly 50 percent. What's more, oddly enough, consumers found the staff to be harder-working and more knowledgeable than when the store gave off no scent. One kitchen appliance chain I know of decided to pump out the fragrance of just-baked apple pie. Sales, not surprisingly, have gone up 33 percent.

What aroma do you most associate with movie theaters? I doubt whether it's the smell of celluloid or of other people. Nope, it's popcorn. The smell of popping corn (and butter) has become so strongly linked with moviegoing that if it weren't there you would more than likely think, *Where am I*? One cinema owner in Chicago opted to install vents on the street outside his theater, piping the popcorn smell out onto the sidewalk a half-hour before the movie was scheduled to begin. Later, he told me, that magically evocative smell helped him fill seats in a matter of minutes.

To be honest, the distinctive fragrance of popcorn, the texture and sound of crunching cornflakes, or the one-of-a-kind smell of a new car has little to do with the actual product, or for that matter its performance. Yet these components have come to play a core role in our relationship with these products. The sensory stimulation not only makes us behave in irrational ways, it also helps us differentiate one product from the next. Sensory stimuli get embedded in our long-term memories; they become part of our decision-making processes.

Glance down at what you're reading: black letters on a white page. That's all I have at my disposal to convince you of a world that can be enhanced not just by vision, but by every other sense we have at our disposal. Imagine a world devoid of color where everything we see is in black and white. Now try to explain the color "red" to a person who has only black-and-white vision. A challenge, to say the least. One no different than the ones confronting brands, because ultimately brands will have to migrate from the tradition and safety of their two-dimensional track, and begin thinking how best to navigate in a Technicolor, Sensurround world. It may be a giant step for the advertising world, but it's an essential leap if advertisers want to be enduring players in this new arena of sensory experience.

The thing is, it's already begun. As far back as 1973, Singapore Airlines broke through the barriers of traditional branding with their Singapore Girl—a move that would prove so successful that in 1994, the Singapore Girl not only celebrated her twenty-first "birthday," but also became the first "brand figure" to be displayed at Madame Tussaud's celebrated Wax Museum in London. Before the Singapore Girl came along, the airline focused promotions exclusively on cabin design, food, comfort, and pricing—bypassing the complete sensory experience potentially at their disposal.

Singapore Airlines shifted strategies by introducing a campaign that was based on the emotional experience of air travel. Was Singapore Airlines just another airline? No—from now on, they would be an entertainment company! In the process, Singapore Airlines invented and rolled out an entirely new array of branding tools. The airline scrapped their old staff uniforms and replaced them with ones made from the finest silk. The fabric design itself was based on the patterns in the cabin décor. Staffers were primped and styled all the way down to their makeup. Stewardesses were offered only two choices of color combinations based on a specific palette designed to blend in with Singapore Airline's brand color scheme (which was defined clearly in the company's internal grooming manual).

On most airlines, many details are left to chance. But Singapore Airlines distinguishes itself by its vigilant attention to detail—often to a bizarre degree. Once I was flying on the airline. It was a long trip and I was bored. Dinner had just been served and distracted, I started, well, playing around with my empty plate that, not surprisingly, was adorned with the Singapore Airlines logo. I swiveled the plate ten degrees to the right. No big deal, right? Wrong. A few minutes later, a Singapore Airlines hostess approached me and gently and wordlessly swiveled my plate back to its original position. Then she vanished. Like a little kid defying an authority figure, I swiveled the plate again. The same thing happened—the hostess appeared out of nowhere and moved it back to its original position. Naturally, I couldn't help but ask her why. Her answer? Singapore Airlines has a manual for everything, including how and where the dinnerware should be placed. If it's off by even an inch, the staffer in charge receives a warning. The second time, he or she is grounded—and has to retake the airline's training program. The third time? By then I was too freaked out even to ask.

No wonder it didn't take long for the Singapore Girl to become an international icon—which naturally trickled down to the airline's hiring standards. The criteria for staff membership were stringent and borderline-inflexible. The members of the cabin crew had to be females under twenty-six years of age. Their makeup had to follow an exacting Pantone manual designed by the airline's marketing department. Their bodies had to fit a made-to-order uniform. Their good looks had to compare positively to the models the airlines used in their print and TV advertising. Candidates not only had to "look" the Singapore Airlines brand, they had to "act" the brand—which included strict instructions on how to address passengers, how to move about in the cabin and how to serve food. (Even the announcements from the captain were carefully scripted by the advertising agency.) The airline went so far as to carry out random body-mass index tests. They literally had a person aboard a plane measuring their employees' weights! If an airline hostess was too shapely, she was grounded.

Politically incorrect as this may come across in many countries, Singapore Airlines was driven by an aim to establish a true sensory brand experience which went well beyond what the typical airline passenger sees and hears.

The sensory branding of the Singapore Girl reached its zenith by the end of the 1990s, when Singapore Airlines introduced Stefan Floridian Waters. Not your average household name to be sure, but Stefan Floridian Waters happens to be an aroma specifically designed as part of Singapore Airlines' brand. Stefan Floridian Waters not only created the fragrance in the flight attendants' perfume, it was blended into the hot towels served before takeoff and generally permeated Singapore Airlines's entire fleet. This patented fragrance has since become an unmistakable, distinct trademark of Singapore Airlines.

Curiously, when asked to describe it, very few people can recall or summon the fragrance. Those who can, describe it as smooth, exotically Asian, with a distinct aura of the feminine. But if you were to ask travelers who take a subsequent journey with Singapore Airlines about this fragrance, all report instant recognition upon stepping into the airplane (I once got an email from a man who told me it transported him back to a Singapore Airlines flight when he and his wife disappeared into the rest room and . . . you can guess the rest). Imagine: a fragrance that can potentially kick-start a kaleidoscope of smooth, comfortable, turbulence-free, and even sensual memories—all reflecting the Singapore Airlines brand.

Brand Bland

It was only around fifty years ago—during the late 1950s, in fact—when the first documented evidence on the positive effects of branding was published. Back then it appeared that consumers were prepared to pay more for branded products—even if the nonbranded item was of the same quality, appearance, and taste. It's hard to believe, but most if not all of the knowledge we have today about branding has its roots in the 1950s and 1960s.

The intense focus on constructing a brand around its "personality"—namely, giving a car or a computer or a designer shirt values, feelings, and associations in order to distinguish it from its rivals—evolved in the 1970s and 1980s. Since then, there have been few if any earth-shattering changes in how consumers perceive brands. Even the Internet still uses banner ads as its primary tool of advertising, even though these ads lack any true interactive foundation. Is this tactic remotely different from showing slides of a smiling local butcher, banker, or florist in a movie theater before the previews start? Honestly—who in the audience is sitting there in the dark with an illuminated pen and paper, assiduously writing down the phone numbers and addresses scrolling across these tedious slides? It's a textbook illustration of the wrong-headed use of media.

There is little doubt that the marketing community is technologically and creatively more sophisticated in its execution of television commercials, print ads, billboards, and radio promotions. But all the communication techniques in use today have one thing in common: they're all based on two senses—sight and sound. That, again, flies in the face of the fact that human beings have three additional senses that can be addressed.

Do You Hear Me, Hear Me, Hear Me . . .

Repetition has been one of the most prominent techniques used by advertisers to ensure that consumers understand and remember a given message. On average, a consumer will see or hear a classic TV campaign three times (incidentally, it doesn't matter where—a bedroom, a kitchen, an airport—the consumer has access to commercial television). It probably goes without saying that the more often a message is repeated, the better consumers remember it. The same is true for a brand. Thus, it's ironic that countless TV commercials use the same forgettable tunes and the same undistinguished voiceovers—ironic because today we know that most of us no longer watch TV ads. At most, we "overhear" them as we make coffee, iron a shirt, tie a tie, read a book, get dressed, root around for socks, check our iPhones, sip our orange juice, or chat with members of our family. Sure, every once in a while we'll glance up quickly at the screen if an interesting sound or message reaches our ears—but that's it.

But if advertisers use the same sounds, voiceovers, and pieces of music, what brand message remains? None.

Obviously, there's a limit to just how many times advertisers can repeat the exact same communications. To what extent can they saturate the airwaves with messages and still expect any of us to pay attention? Watch *any* news station and the screen will be packed with news bars, ticker tapes, stock ratings, and news updates, not to mention a pair of chattering anchormen or anchorwomen—all on a single screen. As I sat in a television studio at Bloomberg recently, the interviewer waited until a commercial break to inform me that viewers seldom paid attention to the channel's scrolling bars of information. "So why do you keep them?" I asked. Because, it turns out, they give TV viewers the impression of money and instantaneously conveyed, continuously refreshed data. In short, it was more a matter of viewer perception than actual viewer need.

The reality is that people are spending less time in front of their televisions, less time reading magazines, and less time listening to the radio. Regardless—over the past few years, advertisers have increased their spending by roughly 3 percent annually, though the figure dropped sharply during the first quarter of 2009 due to the global recession.[6] By the same token, fifteen years ago it was estimated the average consumer received three thousand brand messages a day—a figure that's increased to five thousand.[7] In 1965 the average consumer remembered 34 percent of the ads shown on TV. In 1990 he or she could recall only 14.5 percent.[8] More and more money is being spent executing increasingly less effective—and far less memorable—brand campaigns.

In sum, advertising has hit a wall.

I've Got a Feeling

Shall we go to a movie? Banish the dialogue, the sound effects, and the music and I'm pretty sure you'd agree with me that we're not left with much that entertains us. Alternately, remove the images and the dialogue and simply hum along with the soundtrack. Again, hardly stuff that will keep anyone glued to his or her seat. The joy of movie entertainment comes from the combination of audio and video working together. One sense plus another sense equals not two, but five.

By way of illustration, Bauducco, a Brazilian baked goods manufacturer, tried to appeal to a younger consumer base by piping a chocolate aroma into movie theaters, while at the same time screening a preview for the company's signature product, the chocolate panettone. The campaign proved to be a huge success.[9] A leading fragrance company, Cinescent, gives marketers the opportunity to pump out their brands' fragrance in German movie theaters while commercials for those same brands flash across the screen. One ad for Nivea showed a sun-drenched beach scene, with sunbathers lying on deck chairs and towels. Waves crashed. Seagulls sounded. At which point the scent of Nivea sun cream was infused into the cinema, along with the Nivea logo and a tagline, "Nivea. The Scent of Summer." According to the results of cinema exit polls, moviegoers displayed a startling 515 percent increase in their recall for the Nivea ad, compared with moviegoers who viewed the same ad minus the scent.[10]

The evidence is overwhelming. At what point do we ask, is 2 + 2 = 5 enough? What if we were able to tack on taste, touch, and smell? Wouldn't we be adding more hugely persuasive dimensions? Could the formula be as simple as: sound + vision + touch + smell + taste equals: 2 + 2 + 2 + 2 + 2 = 20? Would we then discover a positive synergy across and among each one of our five senses? Is it the case that delicious-smelling food tastes better? Or that a heavier mobile phone somehow suggests a higher-quality device? Does perfume smell better if it's bottled in a stylish canister? In addition to the audio and visual aspect, won't a brand have more value if it imparts a sense of smell, touch, and taste?

Put it this way: New York-based *Condé Nast Traveler* magazine has named Singapore Airlines the Best Airline. Almost every other independent study agrees—Singapore Airlines is the top. This, despite the fact that the airline's food is average and the legroom is just as cramped as any of the other airlines that make up the top-twenty list.

To what extent can we regard the increased sales in a supermarket that pumps the smell of freshly baked bread through their aisles as a random coincidence? How can we account for the beaming woman in Toys 'R' Us in New York City, grabbing as many canisters of Play-Doh as she can carry, as overhead pumps spray the product's distinctive aroma over the toy section? How can we account for the crispiness of our breakfast cereal "tasting" fresher and better? How can we explain our disappointment when our digital cameras don't "click" when we take a picture, or our freeze-dried coffee fails to make that distinctive exhalation sound when we first unscrew the lid? How can we explain that in one study I carried out, merely the sight of the distinctively shaped roof design of McDonald's, which is uniform across the world, caused consumers' cravings for fast food to rise sharply—just like that?

By the end of the 1990s, Daimler Chrysler established an entirely new department within its company. Its role wasn't to design, build, or even market cars. No, its job was solely to work on the sound of their car doors. You read that right: the *sound*. A team of ten engineers was mandated to analyze and then implement the perfect sound of a car door, whether it was opening or closing. I know, I know, Germans have their precise ways of doing things—but still.

Over the years, car manufacturers have learned a lot about what goes into selling cars. It's not necessarily the car's design or even how fast it goes on a highway. Studies show that interior design—including the way the doors open and shut—goes a long way toward determining whether a consumer will choose one car over another. Why? Because in general females respond more to the feel and texture of the interior than they do to a car's external features. So the way the doors close tends to be an important feature in a consumer's perception of automotive quality. A top car engineer once gave me a fascinating insight: people don't buy cars the same way they did twenty years ago. Today, the average consumer visiting a car showroom first takes a seat in the automobile. She touches the steering wheel. She runs her hand over the seat upholstery. She inhales the "new car smell." She opens and closes the window. She gets out and closes the door, where she hears the distinctive (and artificially manufactured) "clunk" sound. Next, she checks the engine, or rather, opens the hood and stares down blankly at what's inside for a minute or so. In fact, roughly 99 percent of consumers cannot make the slightest bit of sense of what's under a car's hood since the machinery has become so technical and digitalized. What does that little red box mean? How about that yellow one? Got me. After closing the hood, typically she'll scan the car's design, before slipping back into the driver's seat and savoring the smell.

What's missing here? How about a consumer wondering, *How well does this car drive? Is it safe? How many miles per gallon does it get? What's its Blue Book value after five years? Ten?* Now you know why car engineers expend so much effort to create a car's first impression. Because in reality, the engineer told me, our sensual reactions are the only ones we rely on when we're making up our minds whether or not to buy a new automobile.

Daimler Chrysler understands this—so why don't other brands?

Them There Eyes

Sight is immensely seductive—it almost goes without saying. Take the food and color test, which Dr. H. A. Roth performed in 1988. He took a drink, and added coloring to it in various stages of intensity. He then asked volunteers which drink was sweeter. Several hundred students took the test—and got it wrong. They believed that the stronger the color, the sweeter the drink. But in fact it was the opposite: the stronger the color, the more sour the drink actually was![11]

In another test, C. N. DuBose asked the subjects to sample grape, lemon-lime, cherry, and orange drinks. Volunteers had no trouble correctly identifying the flavor if the color matched up. But when the color and the flavor were switched around, only 30 percent of the volunteers who tasted the cherry could identify the right flavor. In fact, 40 percent thought the cherry drink was lemon-lime.[12]

Vision, of course, has much to do with light. As early as the fifth century BC, the Greeks recognized the link between the eye and what they were seeing. By the fourth century BC, Aristotle rejected the idea of a "visual fire" emanating from the human eye, reasoning that if vision were produced by fire in the eye, then human beings would be able to see in the dark. True enough. The difference between our day and nighttime vision is that our night vision is color-blind. To understand truly what an artist sees when painting a picture you admire, consider looking at the subject under the same light.

One of the most revolutionary art movements in history took place when a group of artists in nineteenth-century France who came to be known as the Impressionists began seriously to study the effects of light. At core, their work is a study of the impressions that changing light imparts to a given object. Setting up their oils and easels outdoors, they painted haystacks and water lilies and the like, over and over again. Each painting records a different time of day as well as minute changes in the seasons.

Within the range of visible light, various wavelengths appear to us as different colors; therefore most colors that we see are composed of a range of wavelengths. The eye itself has been understood to work like a camera, in that its function is to send a perfect image to the brain. This in turn has given rise to a misperception so widespread that it even has a name—"the homunculus fallacy (*homunculus* is Latin for "little man"). The fallacy is the idea that when we see something, a small representation of it is transmitted to the brain to be looked at by a little man.

The function of the visual system is to process light patterns into information useful to the organism. Human beings have surprisingly low visual acuity (resolution) in parts of the visual field that are not at the center of where we are looking. We're seldom aware of this, as we typically move our center of gaze to whatever we want to look at.

Light passes through the pupil, and the lens focuses the image on the retina, a sheet of layers of neutral tissue that lines the back of the eyeball.

There are photoreceptors in the first layers of the retina that have light-absorbing chemicals. The signals pass through the first layer to the ganglion cells, which send their signal from the eye via the optic nerve to the brain. This then translates into what we see—a child, a daisy, a carousel, an umbrella, a litter of puppies.

Having said that, all of us see differently. Half-full or half-empty. You say orange, I say vermilion. Sight, as they say, is truly in the eye of the beholder—which is why companies like the renowned authority Pantone specialize in developing tools to help designers communicate colors.

The Visual Brand

Let's examine the Coca-Cola brand from a sheerly visual standpoint. Coke has (to say the least) a very unambiguous sense of color. Quite simply, wherever there's Coke, there's red and white. The company takes its colors extremely seriously. Did you know that Santa Claus traditionally wore green until Coca-Cola began to promote him heavily in the 1950s? Now in every shopping mall across the western world, Santa wears the colors of Coke. The consistent use of the colors, Coke's dynamic ribbon, Coke's typography, and Coke's logo have established an unmistakably clear image which has survived decades and is unmistakable to anyone who's ever been exposed to the brand.

We're All Ears

When I was a child, I remember a day when my classmates and I were asked to sit silently in a circle on the floor and do nothing but listen for two minutes. There were no eventful or outsized sounds, no jazz or classical music playing, just . . . silence. Yet when asked, all of us could recall hearing *something*. And each of us heard something different. For some it was a cough, for others it was a footstep, or a door slamming. Traffic. Leaves rustling. I heard a clock ticking.

Children's hearing is far more acute than adults'. They can recognize, and easily recognize, a far wider variety of noises, too. As we grow older, we lose our auditory sensitivity, as anyone who's had his or her eardrums blasted by an iPod can tell you.

As smell is connected to memory, sound is connected to mood. Sound in fact *creates* mood, as well as feelings and emotions. Would *Love Story* or *The Notebook* be nearly as emotional if you watched them with the sound off?

Just like the vibrations of a drum, or the ripples on a lake, sound originates from the motion or vibration of an object—a motion that sends vibrations or sound waves through the air. The outer ear funnels these vibrations into the ear canal, which move by a process similar to Morse code until they reach the eardrum—which then sets off a chain-link of vibrations. The eardrum vibrates against the three smallest bones in the body, moving the sound through an oval window into the ear's labyrinth, a maze of winding passages. At the front of the labyrinth is a coiled tube, resembling a snail's shell. Here, approximately 25,000 receptors pick up the signals and send them to the brain—the result being we "hear."

Many claim that the loss of hearing is worse than the loss of sight. In a letter from 1910, Helen Keller wrote, "The problems of deafness are deeper and more complex, if not more important, than those of blindness. Deafness is a much worse misfortune. For it means the loss of the most vital stimulus—the sound of the voice that brings language, sets thoughts astir and keeps us in the intellectual company of man."[13]

Do You Hear What I Hear?

The second dimension which marketers use heavily in today's brand-building process is the use of audio. Even though audio technology has been available for over a hundred years, the use of audio still has a long way to go.

Using the same criteria we applied to a brand's visuals, Intel stands out as the company with the clearest, most distinct, consistent, and memorable use of sound. The Intel Inside tune has been around since 1998, making the invisible (and invincible—that legendary chip!) visible via the short, distinct sound used throughout all of Intel's advertising campaigns. Research shows that the Intel jingle, also known as "the wave," is as distinct and memorable as the Intel logo. In fact studies have shown that in many cases people remember the Intel wave better than the logo. Ironically, almost none of us have ever actually seen the product. It's tucked away deep inside a box few consumers dare open. At the same time, we know the sound and the colors, and recognize the logo, all of which transmit a distinct, well-planned message about what's inside—without us once catching sight of the actual product.

Is That All There Is?

Up until now, that would be it for building and maintaining a brand. Drop-dead visuals. Killer audio. Having said this, visit the Internet sites of the world's Fortune Top 1000 brands, and you will quickly come to realize that only 14 percent of them use sound as an integrated element online. Furthermore, only 11 percent of all brands use the strengths of audio in making their brand more distinct, clear, consistent, and memorable.

Consider this: When you open a bottle or can of Coke, there's a distinct, deeply satisfying sound. No one has ever thought to brand this. Then there's Microsoft's start-up notes. Yet Microsoft changes these notes each time they release a new version of their operating system. What happens to the tune when customers listen to Microsoft TV commercials, start up a Microsoft-owned XBox, turn on a Microsoft phone or visit a Microsoft website? It's nowhere to be heard. (According to one Microsoft executive I spoke with, Microsoft's musical signature was "the responsibility of another division" (and thus the reason why it wasn't integrated across every single one of the brand's touch points. Hmm). One wonders why Porsche hasn't branded that new-Porsche smell, or why Motorola neglects to use their ring tone as a consistent signature across every single one of their touch points. After all, 15 percent of the world's mobile phone users listen to their Motorola phone ringing approximately nine times a day.

Jean-Martin Folz, the chairman of the French car manufacturing giant, PSA Peugeot Citroën, decided to adopt a sensory branding strategy to create a sound identity around these two very distinct car brands. Somewhat inexplicably, this sound identity was used internally, rather than for commercial purposes. Every morning, when the company's 65,000 employees turn on their computers, they're greeted by the group's signature tune rather than by Microsoft's start-up notes. The PSA group's tune was also applied to the company's telephone "on hold" music. It went even further. Every time Folz gives a speech about the group's strategy, the music is played as an introduction, before he takes to the stage.

So why not take it outside Peugeot Citroën straight to the ears of the consumer? After all, if Ferrari can build a website where each and every button click exposes Web (and car) aficionados to the distinctive sound of the Ferrari roar, any car manufacturer can do the same.

In the Air Tonight

You can close your eyes, cover your ears, refrain from touch, and reject taste, but smell is an essential element of the air we breathe. It's the one sense we can't turn off (unless we use a clothespin). We smell with every breath we take, which comes to around twenty thousand times a day. Smell is also the sense we most take for granted. When you think about it, there's no cultural activity that caters exclusively to our noses—no sniffing galleries, no concertos written to envelop us with odor, no special menu of smells created for grand occasions, and yet . . . it is our most direct and basic sense.

Ever observed an animal in a new place? The very first thing it does is sniff around. Odors give animals most of the information they need to gauge their potential safety. In fact, once, in celebration of World Animal Day (and c'mon, obviously to boost their sales), the makers of Pedigree dog food placed subtly scented stickers on floors and sidewalks in front of pet shops and supermarkets. When a passing dog inhaled the fake food smell, it went ballistically happy, and baffled pet owners—who smelled nothing—couldn't pass by the stores without seeing the window display of Pedigree cans.[14]

As I alluded to earlier, smell is also extraordinarily powerful in evoking memory. Where you may be at a loss to conjure up the minute details of your childhood home, a whiff of homemade bread can instantly transport you back in time. As Diane Ackerman writes in her lyrical study, *A Natural History of the Senses*, "Hit a tripwire of smell, and memories explode all at once. A complex vision leaps out of the undergrowth."[15]

Few writers have managed to describe the nose more elegantly than Lyall Watson. In *Jacobson's Organ*, his comprehensive and idiosyncratic study of smell, he refers to smell as a "chemical sense." He goes on to explain, "Receptor cells in the nose translate chemical information into electrical signals. These travel along olfactory nerves into the cranial cavity, where they gather in the olfactory bulbs. These, in turn feed the cerebral cortex, where association takes place and nameless signals become transformed into the fragrance of a favorite rose or the musky warning of an irritable skunk."[16]

Smell is nearly impossible to describe in words—which is why we often "borrow" from the wider vocabulary of food and taste to describe a scent. Watson points out how scant the vocabulary for auxiliary odors (such as the way a home or a cupboard might smell) is across all cultures. "In Central Africa alone, auxiliary odors are described as phosphoric, cheesy, nutty, garlicky, rancid, ammoniac, and musky."[17] Once, when visiting Africa, I had the pleasure of meeting up with a highly idiosyncratic local tribe. I learned that when first accepted into the tribe, members would remove their clothing, give away all their belongings, and then don a distinct brown cloth. Members were also asked to discard their given names. So how did these tribespeople identify one another? Via their sense of smell. Without realizing it, all of us release a distinct odor. For those with highly trained noses, such as these tribespeople, names were given out based on the individual's smell.

How we perceive body odor is, as I've just demonstrated, culturally determined. Some Mexicans still believe that the smell of a man's breath is more responsible for conception than his semen. In Japan, 90 percent of the population has no detectable underarm odor, and young men who are unfortunate enough to belong to the odorous minority can be disqualified from military service on these grounds alone. Napoleon famously had no such problem. He wrote to Josephine, "I will be arriving in Paris tomorrow evening. Don't wash."[18] George Orwell did not share Napoleon's passion, and almost a century later wrote, "The real secret of class distinction in the West can be summed up in four frightful words . . . *the lower classes smell.*"[19]

Jack Holly, a U.S. Marine who led patrols in Vietnam says, "I am alive because of my nose. You couldn't see a camo bunker if it was right in front of you. But you can't camouflage smell. I could smell the North Vietnamese before hearing or seeing them. Their smell was not like ours, not Filipino, not South Vietnamese, either. If I smelled that again, I would know it."[20]

Aroma Wasn't Built in a Day

If you agree with me this far, I'm sure you'll be even more surprised to learn how few brands have established a distinct aroma;

less than 6 percent in the Fortune Top 1000 list have even given it a thought.

But just as your brand's sight and sound needs to be clear and distinct, so does its smell. I'm not talking about a blast of tomato soup, or roast chicken. I'm talking only about a subtle scent that in some cases is so fully integrated with the brand that you'd hardly notice it. It can even be a *bad* smell! I once worked with a company that manufactured a powerful floor cleaner that smelled so chemically potent that the marketing director decided to change the smell to roses. Guess what? Sales went down about 27 percent. It turned out that for consumers, the nasty smell signaled that the floor cleaner *worked*.

I conducted a well-publicized study among consumers asking them what their sensory associations were with Starbucks. It turns out the top two were (a) the sound of machines grinding coffee beans; and (b) the aroma of sour milk. So I couldn't help but take note that in early 2008, Starbucks founder and CEO Howard Schultz issued a company-wide mandate to close down 7,100 stores for several hours—shall we say—to spiff things up. Including, I have to imagine, the smell.

Don't Lose Your Touch

Touch is the tool of connection; when all else fails, the skin can come to the rescue. Again, such was the experience of Helen Keller, who became deaf and blind through illness. The unruly child was dragged to the water pump by her teacher, Annie Sullivan, who held her hand under the stream while signing W-A-T-E-R into her palm. This marked the beginning of a tortuous, now-legendary journey that ultimately led to literacy and opened up a world of Braille and books that could be read by fingertips alone.

As many people know, the skin is the largest organ of the body. We're instantly alert to cold, heat, pain, or pressure. Experts estimate that there are fifty receptors per 100 square millimeters each containing 640,000 microreceptors in our brains dedicated to the senses.

As we get older, these numbers decrease and we lose a certain sensitivity in our hands. However, our need for touch does not diminish, and exists beyond detecting danger. Basically, we need the stimulus of touch to grow and thrive.

Dr. John Benjamin once carried out a series of experiments at the University of Colorado Medical Center. Two groups of rats were given identical tools for survival—food, water, and a secure living space. The only difference was that the rats in one group were stroked and caressed, the others largely ignored. The result? The petted rats "learned faster and grew faster."[21]

The word *touch*, of course, encompasses a world of meaning. We try to "stay in touch" with friends, and we "lose touch" with others. People are partial to the "personal touch" as an expression of a personal idiom. We feel "touched" by gestures of care and concern, and express distaste by refusing to "touch something with a ten-foot pole." We're "touched" by madness or a bit of sun. The list goes on.

Naturally, touch also alerts us to our general well-being. Pain travels from skin to brain and triggers warning systems that demand attention. Those who feel no pain may sustain serious injury without even being aware of danger. A therapeutic touch can also alleviate pain. Massage has long been a prescribed remedy for tense muscles and poor circulation in Asian countries and over the past few decades has exploded in the West. Preachers lay hands on those who need to be healed. The Japanese have mastered *shiatsu*, a type of acupuncture using the fingers.

So why have most brands neglected this extraordinary sense?

The Brand Touch

Describe the texture of the brand or brands you love. For many companies this wouldn't apply, yet close to 82 percent of all brands appearing on the Fortune Top 1000 list would be able to take advantage of texture if they were made aware of it.

One of the most distinct brands that appeal to our tactile sense is the luxury electronics company, Bang & Olufsen. Since their products first appeared in 1943, they have put as much detail into their design as they have into the quality of their sound. One of their many innovations has been the all-in-one remote control—enabling the user to operate the television, the radio, the CD, the DVD, as well as the lighting in each room with only one device. First appearing in 1985, this invention has evolved to become a streamlined sensual piece of equipment that oozes quality. Despite the fact that other companies have brought in a similar piece of equipment, the Bang & Olufsen remote is heavy, solid, and utterly distinct. This sense of gravitas is duplicated across every Bang & Olufsen product line, from telephones to speakers, including earphones and the whole range of accessories.

On the Tip of Our Tongues

Taste is detected by special structures called taste buds. It is generally believed that girls are more sensitive to taste than boys—because in fact, girls *do* have more taste buds than boys. That said, human beings have about ten thousand taste buds, mostly concentrated on the tongue, with some at the back of the throat and on the palate. Everyone perceives taste differently. As you get older, your sense of taste changes, and becomes less acute, making it more likely that you will enjoy foods that you considered "too strong" as a child.

There are four types of taste buds, each one sensitive to sweet, salty, sour, and bitter chemicals respectively. Different taste areas of the tongue are better than others at detecting certain flavors, because each type is concentrated in different regions of the tongue. The very tip is best at sweet things (noted in a child's preference to lick a lollipop or an ice cream cone rather than chew it), sour on the sides, bitter at the back, and salty all over. What we think of as "taste" derives from the mixture of these basic elements. Different tastes are distinguished both by smell and by various combinations of flavor.

So where do our taste preferences come from? Americans are born loving sugar—childhood sweets tuned our taste buds early on—but "bitter" is a taste many of us learn to accommodate throughout our lives, and is generally appreciated far more outside the United States.

As a child, I remember once taking a school excursion to a large snack factory in Denmark. As we walked by the shaped corn rings, I snuck a few into my mouth. Having expected that delicious, familiar cheesy flavor, I was confused when I tasted nothing. Literally nothing. All I experienced was a strange texture in my mouth. I then discovered that the snack had to undergo a flavoring process before it was packaged. To this day I remember that horrific blandness—which has served to remind me of the importance of taste.

Losing your sense of taste often generates deep depression. A friend of mine suffering from this phenomenon told me that she would live without any of her senses—but taste. Taste goes hand-in-hand with smell, and if you lack the capacity to taste, all that's left of, say, a plate of fettuccine Alfredo is the texture and temperature of the food. Those who suffer such a loss report that the sensation is akin to forgetting how to breathe. We take smell and taste for granted, unaware that everything around us has a smell—that is, until nothing smells at all.

As I said, taste and smell are closely related. It would not be incorrect to assume that people smell more flavors than they taste. When the nose fails, say from a bad cold, taste suffers an 80 percent loss. Loss of taste without loss of smell is pretty uncommon. Want to savor and enjoy a full sensory appreciation of food? Then note its appearance, its consistency, and its temperature. The author of a respected British medical journal believes that if doctors got closer to their patients, they could smell the ailment. He believes that certain illnesses exude certain odors: a patient who smells like whole-wheat bread may have typhoid, and an apple fragrance just may indicate gangrene.

Most of the descriptive terms and phrases we have for smell are associated with food. Smell is estimated to be ten thousand times more sensitive than taste—rendering taste the weakest of our five senses.

Flaming Lips

Apart from the food and beverage industry, taste is a tricky, elusive sense for most brands to incorporate. However, brands that can incorporate taste can clearly enrich the power of their brand. The fact is, close to 18 percent of the Fortune Top 1000 brands could add taste to their brands, yet almost none have so much as given taste a cursory glance.

Colgate, which unlike many other toothpaste brands, has patented its distinct toothpaste taste, is one of the few exceptions. Yet to date, they haven't extended this distinct taste to their other products, including their toothbrushes or dental flosses. So although they've been totally consistent with establishing the Colgate "look" across their product lines, they've been inconsistent by failing to build their unique taste into products other than toothpaste.

Still, Colgate probably ranks as one of the few companies that apply a distinct taste to their signature product, although there remains a fair bit of room to still incorporate taste as the brand seeks greater traction among consumers.

The taste of Colgate toothpaste, the superbly designed Bang & Olufsen remote control, the Intel digital sound wave, and Coca-Cola's distinctive red and white color scheme all have one thing in common: they've all created a potent third dimension to their product. Their strong sensory uniqueness is distinct enough for users to recognize them without the usual logo or typography cues.

Your Signature, Please

Have you ever heard the expression, "signature dish"? It is the term used by chefs to describe a specific meal for which they're best-known. Over time they may enhance it, add a little spice here, or an additional herb there, but basically, it's the entree with which they're best associated.

This phenomenon is fascinating not only because it permits chefs to create their own niche in a highly competitive market, but it also leads to other dishes related to the primary or "signature" dish. Customers return to the restaurant because they know that everything on the menu will be in harmony with the signature dish. Everything about the surroundings also plays a role: the décor, the manner in which the wait-staff serves the food, the plates, the feel and clink of the cutlery, and the overall attitude of the staff. The food itself? It's only one element of the overall sensory package. What makes a dish truly memorable is the synergy that exists between the various elements of the entire sensory package. If the chef were appealing only to taste and aroma, it's doubtful if the restaurant would attract many repeat visitors.

The effects of sensory branding are astounding. Yes, it's possible to create a truly spectacular commercial, or an advertising jingle you can't get out of your head, but their efficacy is doubled when the two elements are combined. Want to triple, even quadruple, this same effect? Include any and all of our other senses.

This total sensory symphony produces a domino effect. In the way impressions are stored in the brain, if you trigger one sense it will lead to another, then another . . . at which point an entire vista of memories and emotions will instantaneously unfold. Succeeding with two elements is only half a story; creating a synergy across the senses is, or should be, the goal of *every* brand on earth.

A Smashing Effect!

So the idea of sensory branding sounds good in theory? Well, practical steps need to be taken in order to transform a brand into a multisensory experience. The creation of a sensory brand is nothing if not a complex process. Each step is designed in such a way that a brand doesn't lose its identity. It will ensure that companies don't misrepresent the brand, and most importantly, that they won't end up with a situation where the brand fails to fulfill the promises it makes.

Smashing Your Brand

In 1916 a designer from the Root Glass Company of Terre Haute, Indiana was asked to design a glass bottle. His instructions were straightforward: design a bottle whose pieces (even the shards), when broken would still be recognizable as part of the whole. He did as he was asked. The bottle he designed was the classic Coke bottle, one of the most famous glass icons ever. The bottle is still in service, still recognizable, and has been passing the smash test for every generation for nearly a century.

The Coke bottle story reveals a fascinating aspect from a brand-building perspective, because in theory all brands should be able to pass an identical test. Think about it: if a company removed the logo from its brand, would it still be recognizable? Could you still recognize an Apple computer if the word "Apple" was missing? In the middle of an interview I was once giving in a TV studio in Northern Europe, the show's producer brought out a computer—an Apple laptop whose logo had been taped over with a blank sticker. In front of a live audience, the interviewer remarked suddenly that his TV station never accepted product placement or promoted brands. Well, I couldn't let *that* pass. I grabbed the MacBook, held it up to the studio audience and asked them (on a count of three) to shout out the name of the brand. Needless to say, they all screamed out, "Apple!" What about a box of Triscuits, a Harley-Davidson motorcycle, a Ferrari, or a box of Marlboros? Would the colors, graphics, and images standing alone pass the so-called "Smash" test?

It's an interesting exercise to contemplate. Two black ears from a well-known mouse are instantly recognizable as Disney. A Singapore Girl suggests Singapore Airlines. What about a black-and-white photograph of a trim, muscular, handsome young hunk with six-pack abs? Abercrombie & Fitch, of course. These are only components of the brand, and yet they're unmistakable.

The trick is to create each element so that it's so strong, so able to stand alone, yet at the same time so well-integrated that it can take the brand to a whole new level of familiarity.

Who Do You Think You Are Anyway?

In order to successfully smash a brand, a company needs to have an intimate understanding of what it's actually made up of. What are the drivers behind the visual strategy? What is the theory behind the sound? What role does aroma play in the message? How can a company convey its tactile sense on a television screen? How does the thing taste (admittedly, this won't work with mobile phones, TVs, computers)?

Once a company has broken its brand down to its various parts, it's time to reassemble the pieces in such a way that each sensory component is enhanced and can stand alone.

So far the number of true sensory branding cases across the globe can be counted on one hand. Part of the Brand Sense project has been to explore the details of what makes a successful multisensory brand. Can a product really take advantage of all five of our senses? What combination of senses works best together? How do you transfer an emotion communicated by one sense to another? Are consumers turned on by this, or turned off?

A Ringing Success: Nokia

Nokia currently boasts an astounding 40 percent *global* market share in mobile phones. This translates into 400 million people who are chattering away on their Nokia phones on a daily basis. Besides the more obvious elements that characterize Nokia phones, their less obvious branding tools have created what Nokia has become today. According to the brand consultant Interbrand, Nokia is the world's eighth most valuable brand, and it is estimated to be worth $35.9 billion.

The China Syndrome

The sound language of Nokia is only part of their invincible brand story. Add their navigation and user interface and you realize just how conversant you've become with that Nokia in your pocket.

Several months ago, a friend of mine set out to mess with my head by changing the language on my Nokia phone from English to Mandarin. At first I was taken by surprise when every icon on the screen appeared in Chinese letters. However, my familiarity with the Nokia system was such that I felt I could actually read Chinese. I intuitively found my way to the language function where I proceeded to reprogram it back to English. The language of choice played almost no role in my ability to navigate. It was in fact the Nokia language that seamlessly carried me across the cultural divide.

This is a scenario that only a serious market leader can create. Nokia has established its position by consistently educating its consumers. Nokia users are thoroughly familiar with the interface. Any Nokia user can find the most vital functions on their cell phone without even thinking about it. This, you may say, has more to do with luck than with any calculated loyalty building. Not so. Think about it. How often have you been frustrated by a new video machine, microwave, or dishwasher? Even if you've purchased a familiar brand, the new operating system often proves so challenging you feel like tearing your hair out.

Habit plays a large part in creating brand loyalty—a fact many of us may not even realize. In one of the Brand Sense surveys, we asked respondents to choose between a Nokia and a Sony Ericsson phone. One respondent clearly admired the Sony Ericsson for its lightweight and stylish features, but he ultimately chose Nokia because, quite simply, it felt easier to use. This, despite the fact that the Sony Ericsson was cheaper, had more features, and was far more stylish.

Nokia Knows That Laziness Builds Brands

In contrast with almost every other cell phone manufacturer, Nokia has used its opportunity as market leader to introduce an almost invisible (yet branded) Nokia language. Note that this language does not necessarily draw new users, but Nokia's penetration of the market via traditional advertising has accelerated and even secured new consumers—not to mention new purchases. Somehow the company has managed to overcome substantial manufacturing mistakes over the years, including everything from unexpected user errors to faulty displays.

Still, Nokia users keep coming back to the Nokia brand. They return because, well, people like the familiar. They're reluctant to change because they're essentially lazy and don't want to invest the time and effort required to master a new operating system.

As Nokia market penetration increases, and Nokia customers repurchase the brand again and again, this creates an ever-greater loyalty that no traditional brand campaign can create. With each repurchase, the Nokia language becomes further embedded into the behavior of the customer. In effect, the Nokia brand language is out there ensnaring the unsuspecting consumer each time a phone rings within earshot.

Come to think of it, if you're a Nokia phone owner, almost every element of the cell phone experience has turned into a branded Nokia experience. Until recently it was almost unnecessary for you to carry a phone charger because wherever in the world you happened to be, you were bound to find a Nokia recharger that you could plug into, be it through a hotel or a friend. If this unusual—not to mention hugely convenient—feature had been a logo, or if the staff was mandated to tell customers of the guidelines of using this universal feature, Nokia would have scored a major coup. But two years ago, Nokia introduced new charger formats, new plugs, and new standards, thus placing the brand in line with every other mobile phone carrier. What was once a one-of-a-kind brand feature was never recognized as one, and is now gone forever.

Highlights

We are all intimately familiar with our senses—if not always fully aware of them. It's only when one of them is missing that we realize how important they are. For some reason, though, the advertising industry communicates almost exclusively in a world consisting of only one, sometimes two senses—the visual and the auditory. The fact is that a majority of the five thousand ads, messages, and entreaties all of us are exposed to every day are based on what we see and hear—but only rarely on what we smell, touch, and taste.

Brand communication has bumped up against a new frontier. In order to successfully conquer future horizons, brands will have to find ways of appealing to the other three neglected senses. Something new is required to break the see-me-hear-me impasse. Superb picture quality and crystal-clear sound won't do it. We consumers will respond to entreaties that encompass all five senses.

Over the past decade the car industry has transformed every feature down to the very smell of the car into a branded exercise. Brands like Kellogg's, the breakfast cereal experts, no longer count on the natural crunching sound of their product, but design these in sound labs. Singapore Airlines ensures that the aroma in the cabin is as uniform as the color scheme, which matches the makeup and outfits worn by its hostesses.

It is estimated that 40 percent of the world's Fortune 500 brands will include a sensory branding strategy in their marketing plan by the end of the decade. Quite simply, their future survival will depend on it. If brands want to build and maintain future loyalty, they will have to establish a strategy that appeals to all our senses.

There are no two ways about it.

CHAPTER 3

A Smash Hit

HERE'S A FACT I'LL BET YOU didn't know: Carrots once came in every color *but* orange. There were red, black, green, white, and even purple varieties. Then, sometime in the sixteenth century, Dutch growers decided to give this root vegetable a patriotic edge. Using a mutant seed from North Africa, breeders began developing an orange variety in honor of their monarch, William I, the Prince of Orange, who led them to independence against the Spaniards. A country with an orange flag now had its very own orange carrot. You might call this one of history's most superbly successful branding exercises, albeit one that was never capitalized on. Very few people who munch on a carrot—and not even Bugs Bunny—are aware that they're biting into one of the greatest missed branding opportunities of all time.

To place too great an emphasis on a brand's logo carries risks. Least of all there is a danger of neglecting all the other potential opportunities to entice customers. If paid due attention, many other aspects may become recognizable in their own right—namely, color, navigation, texture, sound, and shape. Even blindfolded, you know when you're holding a classic Coke bottle. As you read earlier, in 1915 Earl R. Dean, who was working at the Root Glass Company, was given a brief to design a bottle, which could be recognized by touch in the dark. Furthermore, a person could tell instantaneously what it was even if broken.

Taking his inspiration from the pod of the cocoa bean, Dean produced a shapely bottle with ridged contours. And that day, history was made.

Goodbye to All That

Eliminate a logo, and what's left? This is a very important question because most brands are so much bigger than their logos. Are the remaining components easily identifiable as belonging to the product? If not, it's time to Smash the Brand. The Smash the Brand philosophy considers every possible way a consumer interacts with a product with a view to building or maintaining the image of the brand. The images, the sounds, the tactile feelings, even the text on the product all need to become fully integrated components of the brand itself. If a brand can accomplish this, who needs a logo?

To Know Me Is To Love Me

Our Royal Mail study, as I said earlier, cut through media-driven white noise by engaging our senses and by using tactile, "physical" media. No one needs to be reminded that advertising messages are increasingly cluttering our airwaves and print media. The most recent Federal Trade Commission report from 2004 claims that the average child is bombarded by more than 25,000 TV ads, while the average adult is exposed to more than twice that many.[1] As each brand fights to be heard in this cacophony of the commercial world, it's vital that a product strikes the perfect note—otherwise it will be ignored or forgotten. Our use of media has become far more sporadic. As the broadcast media plays in the background of our hectic lives, we've all developed internal filtering systems that help us drown out the white noise.

This presents an advertiser with enormous challenges. As many as 60 percent of tweens (eight-to-fourteen-year-olds) own their own cell phones, and there's every indication that this number is increasing annually.[2] How would your brand fare on this matchbox-sized canvas?

Only a few brands would pass the Smash Your Brand™ test today. Take a moment to consider a brand you love. Again, if you were to remove the logo and any other textual reference to the brand name, could you still recognize the product? Chances are you will find that without the logo and name, your favorite brand would lose all meaning. In order to eliminate the widespread preoccupation with logos, all other elements—colors, pictures, sound, design, and signage—have to be fully integrated.

A Smashing Process

Smash your brand into many different pieces. Each piece should work independently of the others, although each is still essential in the process of establishing and maintaining a truly smashable brand. The synergies created across the pieces will be essential for a brand to stand out.

Smash Your Picture

Since its beginnings in 1965 under the name Benetton, the United Colors of Benetton has developed a consistent brand style identifiable in any size, in any country, and in any context. It was Benetton's goal to develop its own one-of-a-kind personality. They consider their clothing to be "An expression of our time." Their strategy in maintaining this integrity has been to create all their own images.

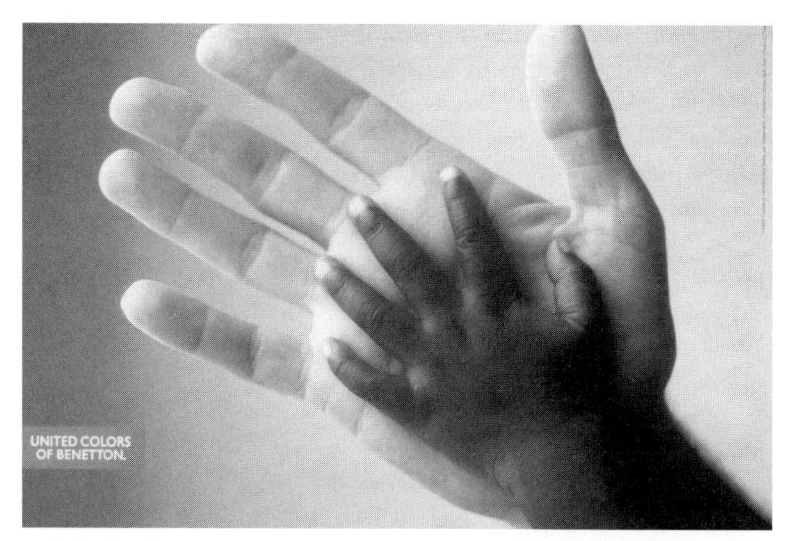

FIGURE 3.1 Guess who? United Colors of Benetton has created a smashable pictorial style totally independent of the company logo. *United Colors of Benetton and Sisley are trademarks of Benetton Group SpA, Italy. Photo: D. Toscani*

Luciano Benetton explains, "Communication should never be commissioned from outside the company, but conceived from within its heart."[3] Benetton is a brand that would handily survive smashing. The image and the design are its own statement and are part and parcel of the Benetton "heart."

Famous faces wearing white mustaches are instantly recognizable as the "Got Milk?" campaign, which has run for more than a decade. From the tennis-playing Williams sisters to Garfield the Cat, everyone who's anyone has done it. You can too! Just join Club Milk and post a photo of your milk mustache on the website. A white line across a lip is all you need to see to know you should drink milk because it's healthy!

Remember the experiment I carried out with the tweens on the *Today* show? Amid our sound and sniff tests, I also created a board collage which showcased a variety of brands. There was a catch, though. The board didn't feature the logos, merely their "smashable" components: Tiffany's robin's-egg-blue box, Coca-Cola's distinctive bottle, Apple's iPod earphones, McDonald's red-and-yellow French fries container, and one of Abercrombie & Fitch's highly sexualized black-and-white photos. In a heartbeat, every single child recognized the iPod earplug photo—which featured no logo, or even the product—and many were even familiar with the Tiffany's box, even though my guess is that most of the seven-to-eleven-year-old children on the show had probably never been inside the store.

Too few companies would be able to pass this kind of brand identity test. Instead, they recycle images, frequently change designers and photographers, and too often many different communication organizations are employed by the various departments in the same corporation. Packaging is done by X, marketing brochures by Y, and public-relations information by Z. This lack of integration fragments the message, making the logo not only necessary, but vital to distinguish a product from its competitors. Corporate brochures are the worst offenders. Nonbranded stereotypical pictures of people in suits smiling around boardroom tables, a towering shot of the company headquarters, and the obligatory portrait of the CEO. I once asked a group of marketers from all across the world to send me the photograph they believed they'd used most frequently in their communications or ad campaigns over the last few years. Weeks later, the results came in—and were they ever scary. Why? Because nearly 30 percent of all the photos showed people shaking hands. Period. Businesspeople shaking hands in office environments, friends shaking hands, bank presidents shaking hands with customers and so forth. I went so far as to create a collage of the photos on a bulletin board, and even began using them in my presentations, at one point asking some of the very same marketers in attendance whose photos belonged to whom. No one had a clue! One can't help but feel the waste of all this energy spent on publications that have nothing to do with the brand itself.

Smash Your Color

Coca-Cola has lost the battle for red in the European market, thanks to stiff competition from powerful local players. Thirty percent of the respondents Brand Sense queried in the United Kingdom consider Vodafone, the mobile phone colossus, the default owner of "Coke-red"; while a smaller 22 percent still associate the color with Coke. Perhaps it would come as no surprise to see variations of the logo as part of Coca-Cola's marketing campaign in Britain. They're duplicating the classic red-and-white logo in different colors—including blue and green—to reflect the color scheme of each and every football team they sponsor. Green is also appearing in Europe and across Asia-Pacific. In Germany, for example, Coke's traditional red screw caps are now green. The trend shows up, too, in the Japanese market, which also regards red as belonging mostly to other brands. Only in Coke's home market, the United States, does Coca-Cola remain strongly associated with red. However, in a majority of the global markets, 36 percent of those surveyed do in fact associate red with Coca-Cola. A smaller 27 percent listed Vodafone (in markets where Vodafone is represented), followed by Budweiser and McDonald's taking a share of 13 and 12 percent respectively.

The major color advantage that Coca-Cola had over Pepsi in the cola wars resulted in Pepsi turning to blue and establishing a global ownership of the color. In the Brand Sense study, 33 percent of the global population associates the color blue with the Pepsi brand. This would not come as good news to IBM, which for years was known as "Big Blue." In fact the results from the Brand Sense study confirm that in some countries, for example, Japan, consumers associate IBM with *black* rather than blue. Only 11 percent of today's consumers across major markets think IBM when they think blue. In fact 14 percent stated that their color perception of IBM is unequivocally black.

True Colors

A quick look at the logos of major corporations reveals that in color as in real estate, it's all about location, location, location. The result? An ever more frantic competition for the very best neighborhood.

In 1942, the cigarette brand Lucky Strike ran up against a problem. The Second World War was raging and chromium, an element essential to the green ink on the company's labels, was in extremely short supply. So at around the same time as American troops invaded North Africa, Lucky Strike released their new pack with its red target, along with the slogan "Lucky Strike has gone to war!" Six weeks later Lucky Strike sales went up 38 percent.

Primary colors clearly have dominated in the world of brands. However, there's no evidence whatsoever to support the fact that red, blue, and yellow are somehow more effective. It seems tradition is the only reason why these colors dominate. Over the past decades, many brands have tried capturing color ownership. Heinz, one of the world's leading manufacturers of quality condiments, launched their "Power of Red" campaign, which aimed to give women the confidence to wear red (and consequently pour gallons of ketchup over the meals they serve). Steve McGowan, the senior brand manager, said, "Our packaging and our brand equity have been built over the years around the 'Lady In Red' concept, which has created a powerful connection between the feelings associated with the color red: energy, joy, control, and confidence."[4]

Switzerland also lays claim to red. Switzerland owns the market on quality watches, knives, cheese, chocolates, and banks. Since the mid-nineteenth century, the country has conspicuously built its brands and made extensive, worldwide use of its colors. When in 1863 the Red Cross was formed, it used the Swiss flag's colors in reverse and, albeit unintentionally, created one of the strongest brands in the world based on red and white. Any company qualified to say "Made in Switzerland" adds substantial value to its brand, given that the country is generally associated with precision and the highest possible quality. Red and white have become synonymous with Switzerland, reflecting one of the most sophisticated state-merchandising exercises to date.

A British telecommunications company decided to position itself between red and yellow on the color wheel spectrum and launched Orange (the company name) in a campaign that proclaimed "The future's bright—the future's Orange." Part of their strategy was to offer students in major cities a free apartment paint job. The only condition was that the color had to be, well, orange. Thus their whole campaign went a long way in laying claim to the ownership of the color orange. Is the telecommunications giant Orange a competitor to the airline company EasyJet? In the UK, the color orange has become the center of a major legal dispute between these two brands, each one claiming the exclusive right to its use.

Yellow is perceived to be the catchiest color of them all. At the beginning of the twentieth century, a telephone directory of services was launched and the Yellow Pages were born.

At around the same time a man by the name of John Hertz held a small stake in an automobile dealership in Chicago with a surplus in used cars. He hit on the idea of transforming them into taxicabs. At some point Hertz heard about a University of Chicago study that revealed yellow was the easiest color for consumers to make out, and so he had these cars all painted in yellow, and called the company Yellow Cab. When Hertz sold out, he went on to form Hertz Rent-a-Car and again made yellow the cornerstone of the new company's logo.

Transport and yellow seem to go hand in hand—go figure. Yellow and red have been claimed by the global express courier company, DHL. It's a popular combination that has seen McDonald's and Kodak wrestling for predominant ownership for decades.

When jewelry is presented in a robin's-egg-blue box, it takes on an added luster because this box, as many people know—including *Today* show tweens!—comes from Tiffany, the New York jeweler, whose name has been synonymous with luxury, exclusivity, and authenticity since 1837. Some brands manage to impart magic and integrity through their packaging alone. Authentic Tiffany boxes and pouches have become marketable items, fetching up to $40 on auction sites. The larger the box, the higher the cost. Large boxes hold big items. One study shows that women's heartbeats increase by roughly 22 percent when they glimpse a Tiffany robin's-egg blue box. I can't help but wonder about the increased male heartbeat rate when they receive their Visa statements at the end of the month.

Tiffany's delicate blue color forms the basis of the store's color scheme. It also shows up in their catalogues, their ads, and their shopping bags. No matter how much money you may offer Tiffany, you cannot buy a box from them. The company's ironclad rule is that boxes (or pouches) leave the store only if they contain an item that's been purchased there.

To date the packaging of only a handful of exclusive brands can be found on auction sites. These include Louis Vuitton, Gucci, Rolex, and Hermès. This is a strong indication of a brand's ability to maintain its equity, as well as a critical indication of its smashability.

Having said this, can attention to color go too far? Try wearing an item of clothing from fashion giant Burberry when visiting pubs in central London, and you may find yourself at risk. British hooligans have adopted the Burberry colors as a form of identification. Rather than emanating luxury and class, Burberry colors are a sign of a community that's looking for trouble. As a result, in certain parts of the UK Burberry has suffered a distinct drop in sales. Moral: never underestimate the power of smashable signals.

Color is essential to brands as it's the most visible (and obvious) first point of communication. School buses, police cars, and garbage trucks first and foremost distinguish themselves by their color. Think mail vans, and the immediate thought is of their color. Using a color in a logo, and then sporadically splashing it across print materials, will not automatically build or maintain the color ownership. However, colors create clear associations in our minds, and these same associations can't help but benefit brands.

Smash Your Shape

Shape is one of the most overlooked branding components, even though certain shapes clearly announce the brand in question. Think of the bottle shapes of Coke, Galliano, or Chanel No. 5. Particular shapes have become synonymous with certain brands. The Golden Arches refer, of course, to McDonald's trademark, and they're consistently present at every outlet in every franchise in every country all over the world. Tab Energy, a new low-calorie energy drink created by Coca-Cola and aimed at females, is tall and narrow, compared to conventional soda cans. Crosse & Blackwell Waistline diet products, a UK-based company, manufacture a series of hard-to-forget hourglass-shaped cans that go a long way toward assuring female customers that if they drink it they'll soon be as shapely as Marilyn Monroe.

Men don't get let off the hook either. The very manly liquor known as Knob Creek Kentucky bourbon is packaged in a large, solid bottle with what the brand's designer describes as "masculine" shoulders. And few marketers can compete with a new brand of Russian Vodka known in translation as "Sexy Tina," which not only contains Irish cream, but comes in a bottle shaped like a female breast (you have to see it to believe it).[5]

Since 1981 the shape of the Absolut vodka bottle has been the primary component in every aspect of the brand and its communication. From fashion shows to ice hotels, footprints on the beach or Northern lights, Absolut's inventive ads are largely based on the shape of the bottle. The shape of the bottle is the shape of the brand.

You'd also recognize a Barbie doll and her body parts anywhere (with no disrespect intended to Barbie). In other words, Barbie, in all her guises, smashes well.

Most computers look fairly generic except the iMac. No matter which generation you're referring to, you could smash the thing any which way and be left in no doubt that the fragments come together to comprise an iMac. iMac would scream out its brand from the splinters of smooth plastic in bright transparent colors, not to mention the bulbous "lamp" design with its movable flat screen. Even the shape of the shards would let you know that the shiny smooth earphones connected with the iPod are uniquely and ubiquitously Apple.

The curve of Barbie's waist, the graceful lines of the Apple, or the contours of the Coke bottle—each element that creates these products is fully integrated into their overall design, making the shape distinctly their own.

Smash Your Name

When the Porsche 911 was introduced in Frankfurt in 1963 the model was dubbed 901. The brochures were printed, the marketing material was all in place—and then, overnight almost, everything had to be scrapped. Much to Porsche's dismay, they discovered that

Peugeot owned the rights to all three-digit model numbers of any combination with a zero in the middle. It was nonnegotiable, too. Fortunately only thirteen models got through the production line with the 901 insignia, and thereafter that particular Porsche became known as the 911.

Peugeot has held the numeric name rights for cars since 1963. The middle zero gives them a distinction that automatically identifies their models as Peugeot—even if you're not able to conjure up a mental picture of a 204, or a 504.

A similar strategy has been adopted by Absolut vodka. They deliberately misspell their brand extensions, using English words inspired by Swedish grammar—Absolut Vanilia, Mandrin, Peppar, or Kurant. Snickers has recently attempted to get into the act and claim a similar visual ID. Candy maker Mars, Inc. has spent a small fortune on a new advertising campaign that takes advantage of the logo shape of their iconic Snickers chocolate bar—without ever once mentioning the name "Snickers." A few examples of what the company has come up with? "Talk Some Snacklish," "Get Dunked on by Patrick Chewing," "Put Your Hunger in a Nougaplex," "Get a Degree in Snackanomics," "Climb Mt. Foodji," and "Take a Field Trip to the Peanutarium."

McDonald's uses the "Mc" in their name to every possible advantage. Their world is awash with Big Macs, McNuggets, McMuffins, and even McCafé coffee. If you happen to receive an email from the corporation you'll be greeted with the words: "Have a MACnificent Day." McDonald's naming philosophy is an essential, unmistakable part of their brand. This has resulted in many a court case like the one in Denmark in 1995, when McDonald's took Allan Bjerrum Pedersen to court for appropriating the company's name (he ran a small hot dog stand named McAllan). This time around, McDonald's was unsuccessful. The court dismissed the claim against Pedersen, and McDonald's was held liable for all legal costs incurred.

The Mac-ization of the language was formally recognized when Merriam-Webster added "McJob" to their collegiate dictionary, defining it as a low-paying job that requires little skill and provides not much opportunity for advancement.

The Disney Corporation has incorporated Disney characters

within the structure of their Burbank, California headquarters. Twenty-foot-high statues of the Seven Dwarfs hold up the roof. Pathways borrow their names from other Disney luminaries—you can wander around Mickey Avenue and stroll across Dopey Drive. By using this naming strategy, Disney has extended its brand across every aspect of their environment.

And let's not forget the brand that practically owns the letter "I." iPhone. iPod. iMac. iTV. Apple, in fact, once had to reach an out-of-court agreement with Cisco Systems centering on which company could use the letter "I" for their phones. What could be more clever than Apple's ownership of a single signature letter of the alphabet? The instant one of its new products hits the market—even if it were an iFridge, an iMicrowave, or an iBook—you'd recognize Apple's fingerprints at once.

The end result of these integrated naming strategies? It reinforces the awareness of a brand's profile.

Smash Your Language

Disney, Kellogg's, and Gillette are three completely different brands with one thing in common. Over the past decade they've established a branded language. The irony is that they may not even be aware of it. Whether coincidentally or deliberately, our Brand Sense study shows that 74 percent of today's consumers associate the word "crunch" with Kellogg's. Another 59 percent considers the word "masculine" and Gillette almost one and the same. An astounding 84 percent of Americans formed the strongest associations of masculinity and Gillette. Must be all those sharp, guy-like blades.

There's one brand, however, that has scored higher in purloining language than any other. It is a brand that welcomes you to its kingdom of fantasy, dreams, promises, and "magic." This will come as no surprise to anyone who has stayed at a Disney resort, taken a Disney cruise, or eaten in a Disney restaurant. It doesn't take long to hear "cast members" encouraging guests to "Have a *magical* day!"

Since the 1950s Disney has consistently built their brand on a foundation that's substantially larger than their logo. A substantial chunk of the Disney brand relies on songs and voice-overs that always include Disney-branded words. Associating words with brands comes at no extra cost. And Disney has managed to "own" six of them:

> "Welcome to our kingdom of *dreams*—the place where *creativity* and *fantasy* go hand in hand spreading *smiles* and *magic* at every *generation*."

The Brand Sense study shows that more than 80 percent—yes, 80 percent—of our respondents directly associate these generic words with Disney.

The key words are repeated over and over again in Disney's advertising copy, song lyrics, story lines, and on the Disney Channel. The words cross all media channels with ease and fluidity. No spare opportunity is wasted in making a potent connection between Disney and Magic, Disney and Fantasy, Disney and Dreams, and so on. In the same manner that Orange, Coca-Cola, and Yellow Pages have claimed their spot on the color spectrum, so Disney has succeeded in staking ownership of the language of fantasy, making it the place where magic happens and dreams come true. What's more, Disney's language survives the smash test. Pick a word, a sentence, or a column from any Disney publication, remove each brand reference, and *voilà* . . . the brand's still recognizable! If you visit London you might one day be lucky enough to spot a car created by Chanel—the perfume and luxury goods company. That said, one lucky owner's Chanel car reads simply, "No. 5."

To create a truly smashable brand requires consistency and patience—a difficult requirement in a corporate world where the only constants are ever-changing branding strategies and revolving marketing presidents. Add to this a fluctuating financial market which demands instant results, and the brand message becomes just another bit of information in an enormously overcrowded field.

For several years Nokia put out the word that their phones were "human"-friendly. They went on to claim that it's "human technology and smart design [that] distinguish Nokia's wide range of products."[6] The company centered their campaigns on its unique "Human Technology"—a phrase that Nokia has even trademarked. Nokia explains that Human Technology is "a concept that is based on Nokia's observation of people's lives, which inspires Nokia to create technology, products and solutions that meet real human needs."[7] Only recently did Nokia decide to downplay this tagline, replacing it with "Connecting People." A very wise choice, it turns out, because in our Brand Sense study, only 14 percent of the consumers surveyed associated the word "human" with Nokia.

In a strategy aimed to establish the ownership of the notion of Nokia as a "human-centered product," the campaign has been less successful. The company seldom mentions the word in its advertising, and so very little confirms or reinforces the concept of Nokia being the one and only provider of "Human Technology."

Nokia is not alone. Many companies have failed to convey their emotional strategy through the written word. For decades Colgate has talked about "Colgate Smiles," so much so that you would imagine that the word "smile" would be firmly in Colgate's corner. Well, not so. When it comes to owning the word association for "smile," Colgate ranks a distant third—behind Disney and McDonald's. A closer examination of this disconnect reveals an intriguing phenomenon. The stronger the brand personality, the more human- and less product-focused it is, hence the easier the consumer finds it to associate words, phrases, and sentences with the brand.

Coca-Cola has used the word "enjoy" forever. It's on billboards, in ads, and even on their product labels, yet Disney's characters have run off with 62 percent of the brand association, leaving Coca-Cola in second place with 53 percent. Likewise, McDonald's Ronald, M&M's animated candies, and Kellogg's raft of characters are also popular associations with "enjoy." As I noted earlier, "crunch," in contrast, has a singular association with Kellogg's.

The companies that take away championship word-association prizes have characteristically created detailed and fully realized characters that personalize their companies. They have almost become the de facto spokespeople for the brand, lending it an engaging human "voice." The point? It isn't necessarily to create characters, but to adopt a human-centered approach, and avoid product-centered tech talk that focuses on features.

Yet as I said earlier, it takes years for phrases, words, and sentences to be identified and accepted as "belonging" to specific brands. Communication has been built from the bottom up, rather than suddenly placed on top as a decorative bit of icing. Typically, effective messages began their life at the same time the product or the brand itself was born. Effective messages were then embraced and passed on from one generation of staff to the next in order to establish their own branded language. The end result? Nearly universal recognition.

For example, there's absolutely no mistaking Absolut vodka's language. The company's Web home page[8] asks the Absolut Legal question: are you lawfully of age to drink? Should you choose the "Yes" option, you are then liberated to enter their world of Absolut Wonder. Once there you discover more about Absolut Reality. Should you wish to contact the company, click on Absolut Contact. Everything on this site is consistent with the Absolut advertising campaign—which has been running for over two decades. It's a campaign that's based on continuity and variety, and seven hundred ads have been produced since 1980, all related to the original vision that launched Absolut Perfection.

The key to forming a smashable language is to integrate it into every single piece of communication that your company is responsible for, including all internal communications.

Smash Your Icon

Icons or symbols are likely to become one of the most important components in rebuilding your smashed brand. We currently operate in a world overflowing with icons, and their numbers are on the rise.

Icons have also been used in advertising to connect symbols, characters, and even animals with a brand. Just think about the Marlboro man, or Schweppes—a soft drink that has used bubbles as its trademark.

Successful icons help companies take their commercial message to new and unexplored terrains. Oh, and by the way? Truly successful icons are also eminently smashable.

Smash Your Sound

Brands, the world over, underestimate the value of sound. A while back I was sitting in a café, drinking a small espresso. Over at the next table, someone's cell phone began shrilling. The ringtone was the well-known Coke melody "Always Coca-Cola." In those short few seconds before the other customer answered his cell phone, the tune had insinuated itself into my brain, where it silently repeated itself the whole day. That certainly says something about digital branding, because not only will the phone's owner be exposed to this catchy Coke jingle several times a day, but anyone who happens to be in the vicinity is obliged to overhear the tune, too.

Brands can be built using sound—not the sound that we take for granted on radio or television commercials, but more like the background music that plays on websites, in stores, on hold buttons on the telephone, or even as ringtones. The Banyan Tree, the luxurious chain of resorts, hotels, and spas that specializes in tranquility and peace for the body and mind, plays the same subtle exotic music in their hotel lobbies as they do in their rooms. What's more, you will hear the distinct relaxing tones when you make your reservations on their website. This Banyan Tree theme is entirely smashable, in the same way the tunes played in the Mandarin Oriental and Peninsula Hotels are (though I must admit, as a frequent guest of the Mandarin Oriental, every time I hear that tune, I associate it with work!). Each of these hotel groups, which operate extensively in Asia, long ago realized that music contributes as much to branding as it does to the overall visual design of their rooms and lobbies. No wonder the latest fashionable brand hotel, Bulgari in Bali, has gone one step further and introduced "soundscapes"—zones within the resort where guests can hear different music depending on their moods, thanks to a Japanese composer who managed to capture the essence (and the emotion) of each of the hotel's breathtaking vistas.

CNN and the BBC World have both consistently used sound as their main brand feature. Does it work? According to BBC World it does. The television signature tune hit the best-selling music charts when the BBC released a special BBC World music compilation featuring all their compositions used as program and station themes.

Qantas, the Australian national airline, released a special music compilation of a children's choir singing "I Still Call Australia Home." The melody of this gung-ho song, which was originally written by an expatriate with emotional ties to his birthplace, played on each Qantas plane while passengers boarded and disembarked. It became part of every one of Qantas's television and radio commercials, successfully creating a strong sense of emotional bonding between airline and consumer, the likes of which had seldom been seen before.

Smash Your Navigation

As a consumer, you may be familiar with a supermarket chain, but unfamiliar with a particular store. Despite this lack of familiarity you probably still feel comfortable shopping there because the internal logic is consistent between outlets, and the store's navigation follows more or less the same pathways. The canned-vegetable aisle is followed by the spice rack aisle, which connects to the pasta aisle, where you'll also find an array of tomato sauces. You can still pick up your gum at the checkout. If you blink you may even think you're back in your usual neighborhood supermarket. This isn't happenstance, nor is it a case of supermarket déjà vu. Instead, it's a deliberately thought-out floor plan that's designed to meet your expectations of the store's brand.

Navigation—the way you find your way around a website, a department store, a supermarket, or any other familiar retail environment—is entirely smashable. If you own one, I'll bet you're able to navigate your iPhone or iPod blindfolded. If at some point you're considering trying out another brand, it may not be your Apple fanaticism keeping you loyal, but the sheer pain of having to relearn an alternate navigation. The fact is, that's branding, too! It presents a challenge for companies to ensure that their navigation remains consistent as their message crosses media channels. However if we use the supermarket model, we know that the vegetables are just over from the dairy products, so even if there's a shelf of cashews in between, we're able to make the necessary mental leap. In the same way, if you're a company, there needs to be a series of consistent links between your website, your cell-phone campaigns, your store layout, your brochures, and your automated phone system because they all link together.

Consistency is the only way to cut through the clutter of contemporary noise. One of the best tricks in the branding arsenal? Good navigation.

Smash Your Behavior

If you happen to visit the Animal Kingdom at Disney World, you will notice the service staff in the jungle next to the tigers speaks in a thick New Delhi accent. In fact every service component has been integrated to match the brand inside the theme park.

Virgin has mastered this notion of consistency, too. Virgin founder Richard Branson conveys a sense of irony and humor via his casual, straightforward, dryly witty communication. The Virgin style, in turn, takes irreverent but good-natured shots at established cultural and business values. With a nudge and a wink to its audience, Virgin creates goodwill and respect, and most importantly it makes the brand infinitely smashable.

At airport check-in counters, there are usually contraptions that indicate the maximum size of carry-on luggage. Airlines ordinarily go to great lengths to convey the legal and safety implications of these restrictions. Virgin does this in its own inimitable way. In a friendly font it lets its passengers know that "You can have a huge ego, but only a bag this size (7kg limit)!"

Virgin's check-in line? Equally painless. Smiling staffers are on hand, the signage is super-friendly, and announcements are often preceded by "Ladies and gentlemen, boys and girls . . ." acknowledging passengers who are all too often overlooked. Even the Virgin flight itself is smashable, and the experience continues after arrival. Signs directing passengers to their oversize luggage wittily point out, "Size does matter!"

Smash Your Service

If you're unhappy about any aspect of a product purchased at Harrods, the legendary London shopping institution, you can return it, replace it, or simply get your money back. No problems whatsoever. The easy-return policy is just one area of service that Harrods has become justly famous for.

Smashing your service is as feasible as smashing all the other more tangible components shaping your brand. Passengers on Cathay Pacific receive a handwritten note from the staff wishing them a special journey. Now, you may give a cynical groan and chalk this up to a standard script penned by a copywriter in the ad agency, but when I was traveling on the airline once, I was taken aback to see that the passenger sitting alongside me received a similar note though with a completely different message. Another time, when boarding one of my never-ending flights, I received a large package from the crew. It read, in part, "Dear Mr. Lindstrom . . . we've noticed you've been away from home a long time . . . so please enjoy the enclosed reading materials." Inside? A series of large envelopes containing copies of local newspapers from my home state.

The Peninsula Hotel in Chicago offers another one-of-a-kind brand of service. When I wished to listen to some music in my room, the desk clerk politely informed me that this particular Peninsula had no CD library. Oh, well, so it goes. Then, minutes later, the concierge called to ask me what my favorite music was. Eminem, Abba, and the Beatles, I answered (secretly wondering why in the world he was asking). Twenty minutes later, I heard a knock on my door. When I opened it, one of the hotel's supremely identifiable (and smashable) bellmen handed over a plastic bag containing three CDs. You guessed it: Eminem, Abba, and the Beatles. "This is a personal present from me to you," the bellman said. "Welcome to the Peninsula."

Now, let's pause here for a second. You've just read this story—as has everyone else buying this book. I've related this anecdote to hundreds of thousands of people attending my conferences, and to millions who watch my TV show or read my articles. My guesstimate would be that some 15 million people have heard this story. The price tag to the Peninsula? About $30.00.

Expectations vary depending on what a brand communicates to its audience and consumers' individual perception of that message. Most companies overpromise and underdeliver. A rare few do the opposite. Louis Vuitton, maker of luxury leather goods, explicitly does *not* offer a lifetime warranty on its products. In fact, the company's documentation states that an additional charge will be applied for any repairs. The salesperson to whom you return your faulty product reiterates this company-wide mandate when you take it in for repair. But, based on my experience, when you come back to pick up your item, chances are good you won't have to pay anything for the service—and a salesperson will assure you this was done especially for you.

Smash Your Tradition

When the debonair James Bond ordered his martini, "shaken not stirred," the phrase took martini to smashable heights. It's lingered in cocktail parlance for forty years, along the way becoming a ritual of sorts. The phrase is but one of the many smashable elements in the 007 spy series, and is echoed in one James Bond movie after another. In each movie James Bond participates in a story line that has developed into a ritual all on its own. There are fast cars and supernaturally sexy women. James Bond theme music is another essential element. Whether the song is performed by Shirley Bassey, Madonna, or Paul McCartney, the sound is first and foremost identifiable as Bond. And audiences around the world can't get enough of it. They wait for the next movie and flock to see it, knowing almost exactly what they're going to get.

But let's stop here for a moment. Did you happen to see the latest James Bond movie? I did. But something was wrong, or missing. As I left the theater, I knew I wasn't the only one who felt that way. But what was it? Then I saw the film a second time. The James Bond franchise had eliminated its best-known, most smashable component. The phrase "Shaken, not stirred" was gone, as was any reference to Bond's signature drink, the vodka martini (it turns out the film's producers demanded too much money from drinks manufacturers for the purposes of product placement, so Coca-Cola stepped in). The famous introduction was gone, too, as was typical-sounding James Bond music. Overnight, the movie studio and the director, Mark Forster, had, no doubt unknowingly, destroyed some of the most smashable components in the world.

The stronger the tradition, the more smashable it becomes.

Another wonderfully smashable theme is Christmas. From the tinsel to the Santas, the trees, fake snow, jingles, carols, roasting turkey, and candles, not to mention the red, gold, and green color combinations—almost every aspect of the season announces Christmas. Along with these traditions come a swath of memories, and brands are often linked to the memories of traditional moments. Dr. Gemma Calvert, a neuroscience expert who operates out of Oxford, UK, and who was an invaluable contributor to the global research study I conducted for my book, *Buyology*, once carried out a research study on cinnamon. Using an fMRI, Dr. Calvert scanned the brains of a group of volunteers—and found that the fragrance of cinnamon was the number one aroma that evoked a joyful Christmas mood. Volunteers' entire brains fired up (including the region of the brain responsible for authentic emotional engagement) as her study subjects inhaled that wonderful spice. Why? Because over time, cinnamon has become for many an essential ingredient in baking or cider-making rituals, which kick-starts an emotional journey whenever we smell it.

Brands need to understand in what context rituals appear, and where there's a potential to build in a branded ritual. Far too many brands ignore the importance of nurturing this phenomenon, overlooking a major opportunity to let consumers "own" the brand . . . and then become its ambassador.

Smash Your Rituals

Can a ritual be trademarked? Apparently it can. Mars did just that when they applied for a patent on the finger-scissors gesture they used in their Twix commercial. The Benelux Trademark Register accepted this, registered it, and now Mars is attempting to extend the trademark worldwide.

Evolving brand-based rituals are proving to be goldmines for brand owners. Take Nabisco's Mallomars as a case in point. Mallomar, a biscuit "enrobed" in chocolate, doesn't do very well in the heat (okay, basically it turns to mush). To avoid a Mallomar meltdown, Nabisco stops production from April to September. But as the weather gets cooler people start waiting for Mallomars to appear on the supermarket shelves. Erin Bondy, a spokeswoman for Kraft, the parent company of Nabisco, says, "When they return, some media outlets told me they throw Mallomar parties."[9] The swallows of Capistrano should be so lucky.

A similar tradition takes place in Denmark. At a specially designated date in November, a Christmas beer called Julebryg, is delivered by horse to selected bars in Copenhagen. But that isn't the only ritual associated with Tuborg beer. Every year, in the days before Christmas, a short, charmingly animated advertisement begins showing up in movie theaters across the country. It features a small reindeer, followed by Santa Claus passing over the screen, all to a Christmas soundtrack. One year Tuborg decided to scrap the ad—it had been running for years, and the company assumed that the Danes had probably had their fill. They were wrong. Where had the reindeer gone, newspaper headlines across Denmark wondered? A year later, the reindeer was back in movie theaters, and whether the Tuborg executive whose bad idea it was to remove the reindeer is still working for the company I'll never know.

In the sports world, we see rituals often embedded into the game. Before the national New Zealand rugby team, the All Blacks, play a game, they perform a ritual Maori war dance known as the Haka (Maori people traditionally performed a Haka before charging into battle). On a less savory note, fans and players of Cardiff City Football Club in Wales have developed a ritual known as "Doing the Ayatollah." The club's fortunes have been less than sparkling, and after witnessing television footage of Iranians mourning the death of Ayatollah Khomeini, they adopted the gesture of tapping the tops of their heads with the palms of both hands every time the team missed a goal or kicked outside of their boundaries. Whether it's performing the Haka or Doing the Ayatollah, these smashable rituals easily identify their teams.

Most rituals are generated by consumers. To date, few brands have seen the value in supporting consumer-generated rituals despite the enormous bonding they can create. Guinness drinkers are devoted to their black beer, but more than that, there's a ritualistic way of drinking it. Devoted Guinness drinkers know that pouring the perfect glass of Guinness is an art form; it takes time and patience.

- Chill the bottle or can for at least three hours. The gentlemen at Guinness suggest between 39F and 45F. Most find that a bit too chilly; 48F to 52F is preferred by most in the States.
- Start with a clean, dry 20 oz. Tulip glass.
- Use the "two-part" pour. Pour the Guinness slowly into a glass tilted at 45 degrees, until it is three-quarters full.
- Allow the surge to settle before filling the glass completely to the top.
- Don't rush it, or the foam won't properly froth. The length of the total perfect pour should exceed two minutes; four to five minutes would be better. You want the head to last for the whole beer.

- Now that our perfect pint, with its creamy white head, is ready to drink, try creating a nice shamrock on the top of the head while pouring out the end of the foam.
- A 20 oz. Imperial Pint glass holds 20 oz. of liquid, not including the head. It allows the regulation 18 oz. of beer, leaving 2 oz. for the head, plus what stands above the rim.

In contrast to most global brands, Guinness is one of the few that has established a raft of strong rituals around the actual consumption of the product. The brand is also closely tied to nationalistic feelings, as well as to sporting institutions. Each of Guinness's many rituals extends from how to order and drink the beer to how a sporting cheer can be recognized by the customers—blindfolded—without even mentioning the name. The brand has emerged from being a traditional beer brand to a position where Guinness has fans rather than customers. The brand manages to fulfill each of the twelve components in the Smash Your Brand philosophy, including shape, color, language, and tradition.

Highlights

Even blindfolded, you'd know you're holding a classic Coke bottle. And if that bottle were dropped and smashed, someone else would be able to tell at first glance what it was.

Remove a logo, and what do you have left? A brand is so much bigger than its logo. Are the remaining components easily identifiable to you, the consumer? If not, it's time for the company to smash its brand.

The Smash Your Brand philosophy considers every possible consumer touch point with a view to creating or maintaining the image of the brand. The images, the sounds, the touch, the text—they all need to become fully integrated components of the product in question (each aspect plays a role as vital as the logo itself).

1. Smash your picture

Benetton is a brand that would survive smashing. The image and the design are its own statement and are part and parcel of the Benetton "heart."

2. Smash your color

A quick look at the logos of major food outlets reveals that colors create clear associations, and it's these associations that will benefit brands.

3. Smash your shape

Think of the bottle shapes of Coke, Absolut, or Chanel No. 5. Particular shapes have become synonymous with certain brands.

4. Smash your name

McDonald's uses "Mac" or "Mc" in their naming strategy: Big Macs, McNuggets, McMuffins, McCafé coffee. Their naming philosophy is an essential part of their brand. Subbrands become intuitively recognizable and tap into the broad set of values that are already established by the parent brand.

5. Smash your language

Disney's language survives the smash test. Pick a word, a sentence, or a column from any Disney publication, remove each brand reference, and *voilà* . . . the brand's still recognizable!

6. Smash your icon

Technology has given us many more channels—which are opening up more and more varieties of advertising opportunities. Icons need to be graphically sophisticated enough so that they can be equally understood on a billboard, computer screen, or cell-phone display.

7. Smash your sound

Brands can be built using sound—and I'm not talking about the sound we all take for granted on radio or television commercials, or the background music that plays on websites, in stores, on hold buttons on the phone, or even ringtones. (In the Philippines, one of the most prominent sounds is rain on tin—it evokes coffee, and makes people thirsty!)

8. Smash your navigation

Consistency is the only way to cut through the clutter of white noise that engulfs our lives. Navigation is one of the most essential tools that can be leveraged in building and maintaining this consistency.

9. Smash your behavior

Richard Branson leads the Virgin empire with a sense of irony, humor, satire, and casual, amusing, straightforward communication. The Virgin style, in turn, takes irreverent shots at established values.

10. Smash your service

How would your customers characterize your service? Unique? Just as it is possible to smash all the other more tangible components, companies should smash their service and still make their brands instantly recognizable.

11. Smash your tradition

The stronger the tradition, the more smashable it becomes. Christmas is wonderfully smashable. So is James Bond. Movie audiences still anticipate hearing him order his martini "shaken not stirred," and the phrase took the martini to smashable heights. Well, until recently, that is, of course.

12. Smash your rituals

Most rituals are generated by consumers. To date, few brands have seen the value in supporting consumer-generated rituals despite the enormous bonding that they can give rise to.

CHAPTER 4

And Then There Were Five

UNTIL RECENTLY, MCDONALD'S hasn't been coasting along as easily as they would have liked. Changing global food trends and lack of service were important factors in the decline in sales recorded in the latter half of 2003. Rethinking these aspects and addressing some of the problems associated with obesity have gone a long way to reverse this downward trend. The next challenge might be solving the simple fact that too many people still think Ronald smells!

A third of the consumers interviewed in the Brand Sense study thought McDonald's restaurants smelled like stale oil. In fact, more than a third of consumers surveyed in the United States were quite harsh in their assessment, saying that their dislike of the smell puts them off their food—and off the brand. A larger 42 percent of consumers surveyed in Britain agreed. The United States and Britain are two of McDonald's largest markets. By comparison, Burger King fared better as only a third of the consumers in the United States, and 30 percent in Britain, felt the same way.

By the same token, don't ever underestimate the distinctive smell of McDonald's. Paradoxically, half of the consumers say they love the smell of cooked food, and a visit to McDonald's makes them salivate. However Burger King again was consistently ahead of McDonald's in this group, where 70 percent claimed a similar positive sensory association with the Burger King brand.

Food trends worldwide indicate that people are becoming increasingly health conscious. McDonald's has taken the initiative in developing much healthier items for their standard menu—a sensory opportunity the company isn't letting pass. To focus only on the smell would fail to paint the full picture of a brand under pressure. Quite a few people—14 percent—claimed the food looks unappetizing. And 15 percent were unhappy with the aesthetics of the restaurants. Consumers in the UK were more damning. Some 24 percent of those affected by the noise in the restaurants said the sound in McDonald's gave them "negative" feelings. Upon further investigation, it appeared that the sound of McDonald's is often equated with the sound of screaming kids, and in some instances with the electronic beep of the fryer timer.

What About Tomorrow?

To a large extent, marketers have operated in a two-dimensional world and only occasionally ventured into a broader universe where they leverage all five senses. It's what consumers want, after all! 4-D simulation games, which include sight, sound, touch, and smell, are a permanent fixture at theme parks and video arcades all across the world. In every major city of the world, sweet aromas and heady scents waft out the doors of many shops specializing in scented soaps and candles, incense, potpourris, and aromatic oils. Aromatherapy in all its guises is designed to help create peaceful and relaxing environments.

As we age, our senses become dulled. Some of our most powerful olfactory impressions are formed in childhood. As I mentioned earlier in chapter 1, children's sense of smell is 200 percent stronger than adults' beyond middle age.[1] Given the fact that children influence an astounding 80 percent of parents' purchases,[2] appealing to our sense of smell becomes increasingly important.

Of the sample surveyed in the Brand Sense study, 37 percent listed "sight" as the most important sense when evaluating our environment. This was followed by 23 percent of consumers who listed "smell." "Touch" ranked the lowest on the scale. Generally though, the statistics that emerged showed only a small differential when it came to a sense-by-sense evaluation, leading us to conclude that all five senses are important in any form of communication (not to mention life experience)—as witnessed in our Royal Mail experiment.

This conclusion comes as no surprise. What *is* surprising, however, is that the entire world of branding has ignored these intuitive findings for so long. Furthermore, our Brand Sense study results revealed that the more sensory touch points consumers can access when they're thinking about buying a brand, the higher the number of sensory memories are activated. And the higher the number of sensory memories activated, the stronger the bonding between brand and consumer.

Almost every consumer interviewed in our Brand Sense focus groups expressed genuine surprise at the lack of a multisensory appeal in today's brands. It's extraordinary when you think of the heights that brands like McDonald's have scaled without paying any attention to, say, the smell of their restaurants. Based on the Brand Sense study, I found that a multisensory appeal pointedly affects the perception of the quality of the product—and thus the value of the brand. The study further demonstrates a correlation between the number of senses a brand appeals to and the price. Multisensory brands can carry higher prices than similar brands with fewer sensory features.

The Brand Sense study also pointed to several other variables that often come into play in consumers' minds. For example, the mention of a car brand could possibly evoke a sense of taste. Then again, this may not be related to anything other than the phenomenon that people often eat in their cars. Some brands might conjure up negative sensory associations. (McDonald's, anyone?) This then manages to negatively impact the total brand perception.

The fact is, each of our senses is inherently interconnected with the others. We taste with our nose. We see with our fingers and hear with our eyes. However, just as we can identify a brand by a smashed bottle, so we can break down the senses to build up and generate a positive connection between we the consumers and the brands we like—and thereby bravely enter the new unexplored territory of sensory branding.

Sound

Sound puts us into the picture, or makes the picture more than an image. As the Inuit asks the visitor coming in out of the cold: "Speak so that I may see you. Add a voice, even a whisper, so that the other is really there."

DAVID ROTHENBERG

When movie technology was new, people sat in cinemas watching silent movies. The theater was never totally silent because these first moving pictures were often accompanied by a pianist playing along with whatever was happening on the screen. It's almost impossible to imagine a modern movie without sound. Sound is fundamental to building the mood and creating the atmosphere of whatever narrative is being told. Sound is hard-wired into our emotional circuits. Did you know, for example, that the muscles in the middle ear of a newborn infant reflexively tighten in preparation for the pitch of a human voice?

Hearing is passive; listening is active. The sound of a brand should target both the hearer and the listener, considering that each one is as important in influencing purchase behavior as the other. While hearing involves receiving auditory information through the ears, listening relies on the capacity to filter, selectively focus, remember, and respond to sound. We use our ears to hear and our brains to listen. Sound is emotionally direct and should thus be considered a powerful tool.

The way a brand sounds should never be underestimated. In fact, it can often be the deciding factor in a consumer's choice. More than

40 percent of consumers believe the cell phone sound—that is, the sound of its ring—is even more important than the phone's design.

In a study published in the *Journal of Consumer Research*, Ronald E. Millman demonstrated that the pace of music playing in the background of stores and restaurants affected service, spending, and even traffic flow.[3] The slower the music, the more people shop. The faster the music, the less they spend. Related studies have shown significantly longer dining times for restaurant tables when slow music was played. This results in more money being spent at the bar. The average bill for diners was 29 percent higher with slow music playing in the background than with fast.

Even if we're more involved in hearing rather than listening, our mood is still affected by what we hear. In a study undertaken by Judy Alpert and Mark Alpert, which explored how music affected mood, they concluded that happy music produces happy moods.[4] However, sad music resulted in greater levels of purchase intent, lending credibility to the age-old saying, "When the going gets tough, the tough go shopping."

The Sound of Music

A fascinating experiment once took place in a small Australian village. Local residents, alarmed by the increase in street crime, got together and decided that the best way to confront the problem was to remove the offenders from the main street after nightfall. Instead of taking a traditional more-police, greater-security, and tough-on-crime stance, they chose to play classical music. Every single block began piping out the sounds of Mozart, Bach, Beethoven, and Brahms. In less than a week, the town reported a dramatic decrease in crime. The experiment was so successful that the main train station in Copenhagen, Denmark adopted the same approach—with similar results, too.

The Bellagio Hotel and Casino in Las Vegas experienced firsthand the power of sound. They took special note of the buzz of slot machines and the shower of coins falling into winners' trays. Great sounds to a victorious gambler, but ostensibly disheartening to the neighbor still pulling that handle and getting nothing but the whir of a losing combination. For a while they replaced the noisy slot machines with "cashless" ones, but to their dismay they found their slot-machine revenue noticeably falling. It seems that a slot machine's not a slot machine unless it whirs and jingles—and this applies to losers and winners alike. In no time at all, the original machines were brought back to service.

David Anders, a gaming analyst for Merrill Lynch, concurred with the move, adding that the tourist market "is not ready" for coinless slots. The sound of coins popping into and flowing out of the machines is part of any casino's ambience, he went on, as it "generates excitement and calls attention to the area. It lets people know other people are winning. With cashless slots, I guess you'd hear the buzz of the printer."[5]

Mood for Thought

Music creates new memories, evokes the past, and can instantaneously transport us to other places and other times. All three characteristics are present in the Disney World universe. Carefully choreographed sound is piped through the entire park. Even the bird sounds are controlled. The entire environment is designed to capture the hearts of children and awaken the kid inside each middle-aged parent. Theme music and recognizable tunes sung by well-loved and well-recognized characters are an essential part of the complete Disney World experience. From the razzmatazz at the main gate, to the up-tempo walking music playing in the streets, Disney's signature songs effectively manipulate our moods.

I once worked with a chain of hospitals in the U.S. that suffered from a crushing medical-appointment cancellation rate. So I had an idea: Why didn't hospital management transform the children's waiting room into a beach-y, summertime environment? We erected a fence, painted pictures of the beach and the sky on the walls, filled the room with sand and sandy playthings—and within a few weeks, the cancellation rate had fallen dramatically. Here's another example: About three years ago, I was working in France with a major bank to evaluate customers' waiting time (the customers weren't happy about the long lines). Within a month, we'd changed the furnishings from dark to bright, gotten rid of all the clocks, changed the music, wafted in a serene, relaxing fragrance—and customers' perceived waiting time was consequently cut in half.

As retailers struggle to find ways to differentiate their stores from their competitors', some are beginning to integrate multisensory components. NikeTown, Borders, FAO Schwarz, and Victoria's Secret are among a steadily growing list of companies using more than just sight and sound. Victoria's Secret, for example, plays classical music in their stores, which creates an exclusive atmosphere and lends an air of prestige to their merchandise. These companies are not alone. Today global audio branding company Muzak has an audience of 100 million people who are listening to branded tunes every day on elevators and across malls and stores—while Starwood's Le Méridien hotel chain plays elevator music that's about as far from a Muzak version of "Let It Be" as you can get. In many of their hotels, it will instead be a "soundscape" that's puzzlingly odd, or provocative, such as "horses clopping across water." Regardless—hotel guests at Le Méridien don't easily forget it.[6]

As I mentioned earlier, sound and sight are the two senses already widely integrated in every aspect of marketing and merchandising. Traditionally, sound has focused on appealing to our hearing, at the expense of our listening capabilities—while marketers have pretty much ignored the notion that sound can actually influence our purchasing decisions.

Sound is becoming more sophisticated, and marketers and advertisers will first need to evaluate what role sound will play in their product or service. Specific sounds are associated with specific goods—and sometimes we as consumers aren't even aware of it. Obviously businesses that traffic in audio will focus almost exclusively on sound. Where sound is an important component of the product, companies would be wise to use it. Even products that have nothing to do with sound can use music as an adjunct to their products. In short, no sound should be ignored.

Because consumers are surrounded by a constant low level of white noise from washing machines, dishwashers, blenders, air conditioners, and the like, many manufacturers once opted for no sound at all. What they found was that by removing the sound, products tended to lose part of their "personality." They also lost a crucial means of communication with the consumer. In the 1970s IBM released their new improved model 6750 typewriter. The beauty of it, or so IBM believed, was that they'd managed to create a completely silent machine. Well, typists hated it. They couldn't tell if the machine was working or not! So IBM added an electronic sound to reproduce the functional noise they'd worked so hard to eliminate!

Good audio design has begun emerging in other industries, demonstrating that sound can add something extra to the brand. Luxury cues are often subconscious. Take for example a car door. How inclined would you be to buy a car whose doors closed with a hollow tinny sound? The way a door closes is more important than you imagine. In the mid-twentieth century when the Japanese were seeking to produce a high-quality car, they formed the first unit whose sole responsibility was to manage the challenge of a "branded car sound."

We need look no further than the Japanese-designed Acura TSX to see just how sophisticated car manufacturing has become—particularly in the area of sensory branding. The engineers methodically refined the design of the door sashes to reduce high-frequency resonance when the doors shut. They also designed a special "bumping door seal" that purposefully transmits a low-frequency vibration to the door itself, creating a sound of "quality."

Nissan, the car manufacturer, is on the verge of introducing a new method of invigorating drowsy drivers. The company's new Fuga model comes equipped with an "attention assist" system that infuses the car with a piney forest fragrance via the air conditioning system to wake up a driver who's been on the road too long and whose eyes are glazing over.[7]

Nearly a third of the consumers surveyed for the Brand Sense study claim they can distinguish one car brand from another by the sound of their doors closing. Japanese and American consumers are the most sensitive to this phenomenon, with 36 percent in Japan and 28 percent in the United States in agreement. Only 14 percent of the consumers across the countries surveyed cannot distinguish a difference.

Sound is given special attention by car makers and it's no surprise that before a product hits the production line, its sound has been created by a multidisciplinary team consisting of sound engineers, product designers, and psychologists who've ensured that the sound of the product will enhance the values and convey standards of trust, safety, and luxury that befit the brand.

Attention to the quality of sound is now spreading across a wide range of industries. Toy companies, computer hardware, white goods, and electronic goods—all these manufacturers are adopting standard sound quality monitoring and are now conscious of characteristics of sharpness, loudness, tonality, roughness, and fluctuation.

The Branded Sound of Bentley

In July 2003 one of the world's most prestigious cars, the Bentley Continental GT, was launched—an approximately £500 million project.

One of the main aims in car acoustics is to reduce noise—noise from the wind, the road, the suspension, and especially from the engine. What's more, the interior should be supremely comfortable, offering the ultimate in driving pleasure. The Bentley Continental GT not only had to look like a Bentley, it also had to *sound* like one. From the very beginning, acoustic engineers decided how the car should sound, and only then did they begin their work in earnest. The Bentley's sound was such a critical consideration that the engineers were able to influence the design of the car, ensuring that both the intake and exhaust manifolds made a true, unique, and instantly identifiable sound.

Bentley carried out extensive research among existing Bentley owners by testing new additions to the brand as well as the sound quality of other luxury sports cars. They ended up with a sound for the Continental GT that is deep, smooth, muscular, and inspiring. A smart move in a market where 44 percent of consumers (yes, you read that right) indicate that the sound of a car is the primary factor in their choice of the brand.

Once Upon a Sound

Today's renewed focus on branded sounds is far from new. In 1965 a famous call was registered. It was broken down into a series of ten sounds alternating between low chesty and high falsetto. Defined in a ten-point description ranging from the first "semi-long sound in the chest register" to the final "long sound down an octave plus a fifth from the preceding sound," this yell belongs to Tarzan. And no one can copy it without due acknowledgment.

The power of Tarzan's call, the chimes of the NBC network, and the well-known MGM lion roar are sounds millions have been familiar with for decades. And then Microsoft's start-up sound for Windows came along. Windows is the operating platform for 97 percent of the world's PC users, which means that more than 400 million people listen to the signature Microsoft sound every day.[8]

Did Microsoft take advantage of the opportunity? According to our Brand Sense study they did—but only partially. Across major markets, 62 percent of the consumers we surveyed who have access to a Windows operating system with speakers recognized Microsoft's distinctive start-up sound, and associated it directly with the Microsoft brand. Consumers in the United States and Japan proved to be the most up-to-date, in contrast with the European customers, who were substantially less familiar with the sound.

Given that this is the sound that a great many computer users hear every single day of their lives, the numbers that recognize it are relatively low. That's understandable when you look at the history of the Windows sound. Since first being released in 1995, Windows has changed its sound four times. The original three-second start-up tune was composed by the avant-garde musician, Brian Eno. His challenge was to create a sound that would be inspiring, universal, optimistic, futuristic, sentimental, and emotional. Still, with all due respect to Brian Eno, Microsoft has missed an opportunity to build on their enormous market share. As I explained earlier in chapter 2, there's a lack of consistency in sound across all Microsoft channels spanning software, PDAs, phones, games, television, and the Internet. Until very recently Microsoft has overlooked the power of sound, leaving the corporation in a situation where they should dedicate their efforts to producing what could potentially become one of the strongest branded tunes in commercial history. If Microsoft continues to tweak its start-up sound every few months, it will take on a generic character in the public's mind, and—trust me on this—next to no one will recognize it.

Nokia's Secret Weapon

These bars of musical notation won't mean much at first glance, but these simple notes have given Nokia a considerable competitive advantage. Give up? It's the music for the Nokia ringtone, and it's been trademarked.

Nokia is the world's largest cell-phone manufacturer, and so millions of tunes are played, and heard, millions of times a day all around the world—which amounts to thousands of hours of branded sounds for each individual.

Over the years Nokia has spent a lot of money marketing the company. But they've hardly spent a dime on promoting its tune—known as the Nokia tune. Nevertheless, the Nokia tune is recognized the world over. Let's do the math. On average, a cell phone rings around nine times a day. The average length of a mobile phone ring is about eight seconds, leaving its owner exposed to more than seven hours of ringtones a year! And this without even considering the substantial amount of ringtone sound that person hears from other cell phone holders. So, how well has Nokia managed to harness this major branding opportunity?

Slowly but surely Nokia has built a significant awareness of their

FIGURE 4.1 A winning formula? The Nokia tune—played by millions of consumers . . . every day!

brand just by taking advantage of something as simple as their ringtone. Our Brand Sense study shows that 41 percent of consumers across the world recognize and associate the tune with the brand when they hear a Nokia cell phone ring. In the UK, this number is considerably higher, with 74 percent recognizing the tune, whereas in the United States, there's 46 percent recognition. It's no coincidence that the most repeated melody in the movie *Love Actually*, starring Hugh Grant, is the Nokia tune. Filmed in London, the storyline has integrated the Nokia tune as an important ingredient when the insecure Sarah, played by Laura Linney, reveals her addictive love affair with a Nokia mobile phone. No surprise the Nokia tune has become an integrated sound phenomenon in the UK.

The Secret Language of Nokia

Nokia has created a spectacularly high sound recognition across the globe. This sound register involves an almost subliminal recognition associated with various cell-phone functions: accept, reject, recharge, flat battery, and even a built-in alarm to wake you or remind you of an important appointment. Chances are you're so familiar with the sound palette that you can recognize the sound language of Nokia without even being aware that you know it.

Based on their 39 percent market share, let's assume Nokia has produced some 400 million cell phones. And assuming that all these phones are still in use, countless millions of people are currently listening to more than seven hours of the Nokia tune a year. This number might be lower since it fails to take into account the large number of consumers who choose other ringtones, as well as the fact that every Nokia phone leaving the factory today is installed with its own default Nokia start-up tune.

Over the past five years Nokia has established a solid indirect branding machine that feeds on our senses in a frequent, highly effective way. The astonishing fact remains that Nokia is not paying one single dollar to secure such enormous exposure.

Here, though, I should add something very important. In *Buyology: Truth and Lies About Why We Buy*, my team and I carried out the world's largest global neuromarketing research study ever conducted. Our volunteers listened to the Nokia tune under an fMRI brain scanner and the results were, to say the least, surprising. The Nokia tune—heard as frequently around the globe every day as "Happy Birthday"—was revealed to be a major turn-off for Nokia mobile phone owners. It reminded them of stress, work responsibilities, and the call they hoped wasn't coming in from the office. Rumor has it that ever since *Buyology* was published, Nokia has changed its tune . . .

Motorola's Search for the Right Tune . . .

Besides Microsoft, Nokia's closest competitor is Motorola. The latter is struggling to achieve the same sort of brand awareness that Nokia enjoys. However an astounding 11 percent of the consumers surveyed in our Brand Sense study mistook the Motorola ring for a Nokia tune. The percentage is even higher in the United States, Motorola's home market, where 15 percent of people confused the brands, generally assuming, however, that the tune was Nokia's. Only 10 percent of the consumers we surveyed worldwide recognized the Motorola ring, including 13 percent in their home market. But these are early days. There are still many sound opportunities that are ripe for exploration.

Intel versus Nokia

It wasn't that long ago if you mentioned the word "microprocessor" you were likely to get a bored, mystified stare. Few mainstream consumers knew anything about the processor, even though it was the "brain" that powered their computers. But today many personal computer users can recite the specification and speed of the processor, in the same way that car owners can tell you if they have a V4, V6, or V8 engine. The awareness of "Intel" has grown along with our awareness of the chip and what it actually does.

Launched in 1991, the Intel Inside program created history. It was the first time a PC component manufacturer successfully communicated directly to computer buyers. Today, the Intel Inside program is one of the world's largest cooperative marketing programs, supported by thousands of PC makers who are licensed to use the Intel Inside logos, and who spend close to $200 million a year on marketing on top of the cooperative marketing program, which is rumored to have a $1 billion price tag. Did Intel get value for their money? Definitely, considering that 56 percent of consumers across the world recognize the Intel Inside tune. Yet it is intriguing to realize that Nokia achieved sound awareness with only a limited investment, while Intel spent millions attempting to achieve the same goal. This makes Intel literally the only product in the world no one has seen, heard, or touched; yet by using sound and vision as the main pillars of their branding strategy, people the world over can dance to the Intel tune.

Every product has a sound. Your Siemens microwave pings and your Miele dishwasher ding-dongs. Your BMW's doors, your Dell computer, and your Seiko wristwatch all have their unmistakable sound. Nonelectronic sounds also pervade our life. Corks pop. We hear the opening of the milk carton, the crunching of our cornflakes, the bubbling of a freshly poured soda. There are thousands of brands that have yet to realize the enormous potential available by tapping into sounds and making them an integral feature of what they have to offer consumers.

One thing is certain. It's only a matter of time before everybody starts making some noise.

Case Study: Bang & Olufsen: Branding the Sound of Falling Aluminum!

Is there a similarity between the sound of aluminum falling onto cobblestones on a street in Denmark and the sound of the ring of a corded phone? A strange juxtaposition? Perhaps not. If I were to sit you down in a room full of traditional telephones, each ringing the ring of a branded phone, would you be able to identify which brand is which? Naturally you would hear the difference from phone to phone, but would you be able to pick the brand?

Whether we're talking about AT&T or GE, Panasonic or Sony, no corded phone manufacturer has designed a distinct, user-friendly, and branded sound similar to Nokia's cell phone tune—except for one which, back in 1993, released their latest model and broke the branded silence.

When the Danish luxury hi-fi manufacturer Bang & Olufsen commissioned composer and musician Kenneth Knudsen to design a unique, silken, attention-demanding sound for the next corded BeoCom 2 telephone, the challenge was to think laterally, and come up with a sound that was recognizably distinct. This sound not only had to be distinct but could also serve as an unmistakable audio logo to brand Bang & Olufsen.

The result is evident. Knudsen combined the sounds of falling aluminum tubes with musical notes, a sound he believes reflects the whole concept of the BeoCom 2. He says, "We call it a ringing tune rather than a tone, as it contains many more elements than a simple note. This ringing tune has an acoustic texture of metal and glass, representing the physical components of the phone itself. Within one second, we wish to communicate a mood, a feeling, an impression; just like you get when you meet the physical product." The BeoCom 2 ring tune has raised the bar in the manufacture of corded phones. By refining this existing sensory touch point, additional brand equity is established, and another aspect of the Bang & Olufsen brand enters the universe.

Poul Praestgaard, senior technology and innovation manager at Acoustics Research, states that the "humanization" element will become standard in all future developments from Bang & Olufsen. This attitude perfectly supports the core value of the brand, and adds another sensory dimension to the identification of the product.

Sight

The question is not what you look at, but what you see.

HENRY DAVID THOREAU

Here's a question: Is it possible to broadcast an entire TV commercial without revealing the brand's logo even once? For that matter, without even mentioning the name of the brand? In the Philippines, Nestlé recently decided to take advantage of their leadership position when they launched a new campaign for their flagship brand, Nescafé. I worked hard with the company's team to find ways to create a TV ad such as the one in question. The secret? To photograph a red mug and *only* a red mug (if you're familiar with Nescafé, you'll probably be familiar with that iconic red mug). Certainly in the Philippines, the brand had attained a nationwide celebrity whereby consumers could identify it immediately with Nescafé coffee. What we came up with was the company's first-ever TV commercial—featuring a mini-narrative of a young man returning from the city to a small country town. His welcome-home drink? A red cup of Nescafé. Without ever once mentioning the brand, this highly smashable commercial played on every single one of the brand's smashable elements, and was instantly taken to heart by bloggers across the Philippines, where it even reached cult status. Today, you'll have a hard time locating the Nescafé logo in the company's ads—at the same time sales of the brand have never been higher.

The human brain updates images quicker than we see. It accommodates every turn of the head, every movement, every color, and every image. In describing vision, Dr. Diane Szaflarski says, "The efficiency and completeness of your eyes and brain is unparalleled in comparison with any piece of apparatus or instrumentation ever invented."[9]

Vision, of course, is the most powerful of our five senses. According to Geoff Crook, the head of the sensory design research lab at Central Saint Martins College of Art and Design in London, 83 percent of the information people retain is received visually. He goes on to say that this is probably because they lack other options.[10] The question remains: Is this fact still relevant? Every indication from our Brand Sense study indicates that of all the senses, smell is by far the most persuasive.

When *Brand Sense* first hit the shelves in 2005, I carried out a series of symposiums across the world. During a session in New York, I had an experience I'll never forget. A woman approached me and told me she'd temporarily lost her sight six months earlier—and at one point had even wondered whether life was still worth living. Yet as we talked, she revealed a fascinating insight. The first month of her new life without sight, she panicked . . . and then something very unexpected happened. Suddenly, after a month she was able to find her way around using only her sense of smell, whether it was the location of her neighborhood Starbucks or the street where she knew to turn right that led to her workplace. She even knew when someone was passing her on the sidewalk (and sometimes even knew who it was!). Gradually, her sense of smell became even more intense, as did her remaining four senses. When she finally recovered her sight, she told me, she could smell, hear, touch, and taste better; in fact, every single one of her senses had improved. Occasionally I'll ask marketers or brand builders to pretend that they're sightless for forty-eight hours. At first, of course, it's nerve-wracking, but just like the woman at my New York symposium, they realize that their other senses grow keener and sharper. (I once went so far as to ask a group of McDonald's executives to visit their restaurants blindfolded. Among other things, it taught them that the company owned much, much more than those iconic golden arches—including smells, sounds, and touch points.)

The reality is that copious quantities of visual information bombard us twenty-four hours a day. Our brains' natural filtering devices kick in, so the visual effects fail to pack the punch that they potentially could. Yet, only a small 19 percent of consumers we surveyed worldwide believe that the appearance of an item of clothing is more important than how it feels. Whereas a good half of our respondents placed the emphasis on feel rather than appearance.

The fashion industry isn't alone in experiencing this swing in preference from look to feel. The food industry is witnessing a similar, although less dramatic pattern emerge. More than 20 percent of consumers claim that the smell of food is more important than the taste. Rather than assuming this to be a rejection of design or long-standing taste preferences, it's more an indication of the emergence of our other senses taking their place in the holistic scheme of a sensual universe. Still, there's no escaping the fact that distinctive design generates distinctive brands, and successful brands are by their very nature visually smashable.

Just as Nescafé secured the ownership of its container (and the smell we all inhale when we open it which, by the way, doesn't exist in nature but has been developed over the past decades in labs to ensure that a wonderfully fresh coffee smell assails our nostrils the moment we unscrew the lid), it's just as possible to secure ownership of a pill. You heard me, a *pill*. Any man who's come to rely on his little blue, diamond-shaped pill will know what I'm talking about. It's Viagra. Viagra is one of the jewels in the pharmaceutical company Pfizer's crown. Former presidential hopeful, Senator Bob Dole, became one of the paid spokespeople of this drug targeting erectile dysfunction. In the ads he referred to the pill as his "little blue friend," and promised it "changes lives for the better."

Viagra is an excellent example of how color and shape can be used effectively, and be protected by a trademark. This combination of pharmaceutical brand identity and product design is recognized globally. By taking advantage of the visual components of the tablet, Pfizer has helped Viagra secure trademarked brand loyalty beyond their drug patent.

Pharmaceutical companies typically distinguish their products by color and shape. Accudose tablets, which treat thyroid conditions, come shaped like a thyroid gland. In its TV ads, AstraZeneca promotes their leading anti-ulcer medication as the "purple pill." None of this is new. Over thirty years ago, the Rolling Stones referred to a five-milligram Valium in "Mother's Little Helper," a sardonic song about females who needed the help of little yellow pills to make it through the day.

Tablets and capsules come in all shapes, sizes, and colors, each intended to differentiate the product, impart a particular emotional "feel" to the drug, and instill customer loyalty. The way a tablet looks is an important aspect in maintaining loyalty. When AstraZeneca decided to replace Prilosec with Nexium, they not only used the same color, but referred to it as the "*new* purple pill."

The Shape of Things

Little blue pills are one way of changing individual lives—but an innovative use of shape can change the life, and destiny, of an entire city. Take the recession-plagued town of Bilbao in Basque country in Spain. This industrial port had long dreamed of revitalizing and reinventing their somewhat dilapidated image. After years of planning and negotiation with the Solomon R. Guggenheim foundation, they hired innovative architect Frank O. Gehry to design a one-of-a-kind museum on a large site in the middle of the town.

Gehry designed an organic sculpture. Its swooping titanium-clad curves house a museum that's so spectacular—and so instantly iconic—that the Bilbao Guggenheim has become one of Europe's most popular new sites. Tourists are flocking there just to experience the Guggenheim's galleries. Bilbao, once just another weary industrial town on the European map, has been transformed by a building, which beckons visitors with its courageous, daring, and totally unique shapes.

Innovative architectural structures often become legendary trademarks instantly synonymous with the cities where they reside. Only Sydney, Australia can claim the billowing sails of the Opera House that sparkle on the foreshore of the harbor. Jorn Utzon's revolutionary design with its organic shapes and lack of surface decoration adds to Sydney in every way—it's a venue for performing art, people congregate on its broad steps, street performers line the walkways, and it offers some of the city's most spectacular views. The Sydney Opera House and Guggenheim Bilbao are both totally smashable.

Shape is an instantly recognizable visual aspect of any brand. When Theodore Tobler designed a triangular shape for his chocolate bar, its shape stood out more prominently than its taste. In 1906 it was against the law for chocolate makers to use their Swiss heritage in their logo, so as a way of proclaiming his nationhood, Tobler used the Matterhorn mountain to inspire the shape of his product. Fearing that a competitor would duplicate his concept, he applied for a patent on the manufacturing process in Berne. This was granted and Toblerone became the first chocolate product in the world to be patented.

Once, when I was a kid, I decided to melt a Toblerone down into individual chocolate bars. But when I handed the bars out to my friends, no one liked them. Clearly the essence of Toblerone—the very point of it, in fact—is that you have to fight it in your mouth, and that much of the pleasure of eating a Toblerone bar has to do with conquering its distinctive shape.

Seventeen years after Theodore Tobler patented his chocolate, Milton S. Hershey registered his Hershey's Kisses, and turned his plume-wrapped chocolates into a cultural icon. Over the past century, an entire Hershey world has been built around the original Hershey's Kisses foundation stone. Every day 25 million Kisses roll off the production line in Hershey, Pennsylvania. It's a town that bills itself as "The sweetest place on earth," a place that's "built on chocolate." Streetlights are shaped like Hershey's Kisses, and there's accommodation, amenities, and activities "in all flavors"![11]

Hershey Park is one of the main attractions. Entertainment day and night. Food halls that serve up Hershey chocolate milkshakes and Hershey's Kisses brownies. You can hold conferences at the Hershey Lodge, stay at Hotel Hershey, and pamper yourself at the spa with treatments like Whipped Cocoa baths and Chocolate Fondue wraps. Sweet.

Chocolates aside, there are many products that have based their identity on their distinct shape. The liquor industry has been at the forefront. Take the distinctive Galliano bottle, which is shaped like a classical Roman column. Finlandia vodka, Kahlúa, Bombay Gin, Johnnie Walker, and Hennessy XO cognac are all products whose bottles' shapes define their brand.

More recently the liquor industry has looked to the perfume and fashion world for inspiration. Coco Chanel loved perfume bottles. She even displayed the empty ones on her vanity table. She was once quoted as saying, "Those bottles are my memories of surrender and conquest . . . my crown jewels of love," and went on to state that, "The bottle is the physical manifestation of the scent it contains, daring, seductive, alluring."[12]

The liquor industry would love nothing more than to emulate some of the hope and promise that perfume bottles communicate—which isn't as far-fetched as it may sound. Packages possess mystery and intrigue. Statistics show that 40 percent of all perfume purchase decisions are based on the design of the bottle. Jean-Paul Gaultier has taken this notion all the way with Fragile, his perfume for women. Fragile comes in a brown cardboard box with the word "Fragile" stamped on it in red. Inside the intriguing package is a magical snowball. Shake it up and a thousand golden flakes dance around a Fragile woman. Close to two million bottles have been sold. No wonder, as today we know that 80 percent of the time we spend making up our minds in duty-free stores as to what perfume to buy is based entirely on the shape or design of the bottle—not what the perfume smells like!

The auto industry is another industry where shape plays a vital role. In many car models, shape has even become the defining feature. Think Beetle, Mini, and the military-inspired Hummer. Within this distinguished, shape-centered crowd, the Lamborghini has carved out its own special niche since it's the only vehicle that has doors that open upward instead of outward. This unique feature is trademarked. No one else can manufacture a car with this type of door.

Distinctive shapes create the most solid foundation for brand building across channels. We recognize and remember shape and maybe this is what accounts for the longevity of Hershey's Kisses, Toblerone, and the Beetle.

Touch the Sky

Joy has a texture.

OPRAH WINFREY

Wine bottles are now coming with screw tops rather than corks. Does wine sealed with a cork taste better than wine sealed with a screw top? Probably not, at least not for any recent vintage. Now, this is undeniably a matter of perception, but irrational as it may be, I imagine the wine that I've just poured from a just-uncorked bottle is superior. The screw top reminds me of soda, and (again, irrationally) fails to assure me of the quality of the wine. The tactile sensations associated with opening a bottle of corked wine are lost. Or what about New Year's Eve at the stroke of midnight? Let's imagine that a top executive at a leading French champagne company decides to replace his corks with screwtops. What would happen? Three . . . two . . . one . . . Happy New Year! But instead of a major pop, partygoers would hear only a sad, subtle, spirit-deflating fizz. The ritual would be gone, the champagne would taste awful, and I wouldn't even be surprised if the year ahead was a disaster! All this from the simple pop of a cork.

How a brand feels has a lot to do with what sort of quality we attribute to the product. People still go around kicking the tires of a car they're thinking of buying. This may have been a reasonable test of quality many years ago, but today it's as irrational as the concept of the cork somehow adding to the taste of the wine. However nonsensical it may be, the feel of a product is essential in forming the perception we have of the brand.

The way a car feels when we sit inside it and run our hands over the steering and controls is of utmost importance to 49 percent of consumers making an automotive choice. Less than 4 percent of the people surveyed suggested that the tactile feeling of a car is irrelevant.

Britain's Asda supermarket chain, a subsidiary of Walmart Inc., has cottoned on to the economic advantages of touch. They tore off the wrappers from several brands of toilet paper so that shoppers could feel and compare textures. This has resulted in soaring sales for its home brand, and the decision by management to allot an additional 50 percent of store space to their product.

To counteract the Florida humidity, Disney World sprinkled chilled water on people hovering outside its shops, luring them into the air-conditioned world of merchandising. In Las Vegas, Coke has installed vending machines that spray a subtle mist in the faces of passing tourists whenever the temperature reaches 100 degrees

Farenheit. According to the designer of this innovation, when the machine begins misting, sales skyrocket.

The tactile qualities of a brand are often not quite as obvious as this bottom line. Perhaps one of the most intriguing results that emerged in the Brand Sense study occurred in the cell phone industry. One would imagine that the release of fashionable cell phones that allow consumers to customize their look and ring would be permanently susceptible to an ever-changing parade of newer, more fashionable models. Well, guess again. Our results revealed that 35 percent of the consumers we surveyed stated that the *feel* of their phone was more important than the way it *looked*. An astounding 46 percent of U.S. consumers agreed.

As electronic goods are manufactured in smaller and lighter versions, so consumers' perception keeps apace. Although heavier weight intuitively feels more substantial, we also like the convenience of small and light. There is one important proviso, however, and that is that the device in question has to be made from quality materials. We don't want our digital cameras to feel like plastic, nor do we want our PDAs to feel tinny. We demand superior craftsmanship with the most innovative materials.

Many electronic goods are going retro. A newer range of digital cameras is taking its inspiration from pre-digital cameras because consumers are demanding more than technology for its own sake. The average size of a man's hand is just too large to feel comfortable and confident manipulating a camera that can fit snugly in his palm. Then there's the issue of shutter sound. These new-generation larger cameras have added an artificial shutter sound that lets you know that a picture's been snapped.

A device as simple as a remote control can tell us a great deal about the quality of a brand. The heavier the remote, the better the quality—at least according to the consumer, who often makes her quality evaluation based on a product's feel rather than its look. This might explain why the manufacturer of luxury hi-fidelity equipment, Bang & Olufsen, added weight to their remote control. They have consistently sought to build the ultimate quality items, but have worked equally hard to ensure that consumers have the best possible perception of their brand. They've emphasized every aspect of their engineering, from the weight of the remote to the way their products open and close to the precision sound generated by the micro engines.

Losing the Grip on Coke

In 1996 the Coca-Cola Company worked on Project Can, which was designed to transform the packaging from bottle to can. By the end of 2000, Coca-Cola had their first prototype ready for production. The famous bottle was about to morph into a bottle-shaped aluminum can. Then an unexpected hitch developed. The new shape of the full can was unable to carry the weight when stacked. The amount of damage that crushed cans and spillage would cause—well, Coke didn't even want to think about it. The project stalled and was eventually dropped. From then on, Coke cans were doomed to share their shape with every other soda on the market, with only the company's signature red distinguishing the brand.

Did the Coca-Cola Company abandon their shaped-can project prematurely? A year later, Sapporo Breweries in Japan managed to achieve what Coke had been working on for years by releasing the world's first bottle-shaped can. The part-bottle, part-can container developed by Daiwa was an instant success. The distinct taste of Sapporo beer together with the unique shape of the can proved a winning combination.

Although the Brand Sense focus groups confirmed that Coke still ruled supreme in shape recognition in countries that sell Coke in a bottle, this is the first time Coke has lost its edge to another brand. But since the early 1990s, Coca-Cola has seen an erosion in the distinct characteristics that were once uniquely associated with their brand.

A Steady Downgrade

When the Coca-Cola glass bottle was introduced with its distinct shape, size, and weight, it became an overnight icon. As the company embraced new technology and adopted plastic bottles and aluminum cans, the tactile associations so powerfully associated with their product steadily eroded.

The dissipation of the brand didn't stop at the can. As sales of post mix increased—that's when the drink is mixed from syrup and carbonated water—and the brand was no longer served in a recognizable container, Coke failed even to be recognized as anything other than cola. Furthermore, in order to secure massive distribution through restaurant-chain outlets, the company agreed to have its product served in paper cups marked with the restaurant's logo. The only way you know you're getting a Coke is if you see the logo on the dispensing machine. You drink it out of a cup marked McDonald's, or Burger King, or Wimpy, or KFC!

Even though limited statistics are available, the trend is clear. Today it is estimated that more than 99 percent of all Coke sold in the United States is served in plastic, metal, or paper—just not glass. The fact is that most consumers in the United States, who want to drink their Coke from a classic bottle, have to make a concerted effort to seek it out.

According to our Brand Sense study, 59 percent of the world's consumers (and most kids, at least those who've seen one) prefer their Coke in a glass bottle. This includes 61 percent of the U.S.-based customers and 63 percent of those in the UK. Despite this evidence, the company continues to decrease its production of Coke in a glass bottle, diminishing one of the company's most important assets. These statistics from the Brand Sense study confirm that the distinct Coca-Cola touch is slipping through the company's fingers. What emerged from the study is that in those countries where the glass bottle has been replaced with plastic, Coke's tactile advantage has been displaced.

Over the past years, Coke has been suffering. Our global study conclusively shows that its major competitor, Pepsi, is gaining an edge on touch. Within the home market, 60 percent of American consumers stated that Pepsi represents the strongest tactile sensation. In contrast, only 55 percent of the consumers surveyed believe that Coca-Cola was distinct. Even though some statistical uncertainty has to be taken into consideration, for Coke that's an amazing five percentage points less than their century-old enemy. A similar picture appeared when we asked U.S. consumers how the old rivals fared in the physical sensation department. Coke led by a marginal 6 percent, scoring 46 percent over Pepsi's 40 percent.

Still, over the past couple of years, Coca-Cola has replaced many members of its team, and begun focusing on the importance of tactile sensation. Today, five years after Coke failed miserably in the Brand Sense experiment, the company is back on track. Even though the classic Coca-Cola glass bottle has vanished from most supermarkets, it still reappears around important holiday seasons, reminding customers about the brand's ownership of what's probably the most recognizable bottle in the world. Has it helped? Absolutely. Today, an enormous majority of consumers claim that Coke tastes better when they drink it out of a bottle than a can. Which is ironic, considering the high probability that few of these consumers have ever seen Coke in a glass bottle in their lives.

Is Coke Prepared for the Final Battle?

At the international marketplace, glass-bottle Coke is very much alive and still kicking in the face of a well-planned replacement process. Wherever the bottle is still sold, Coke emerges as the clear tactile leader in the soft-drink market. In Europe 58 percent of the consumers in our study stated that they still perceive a unique tactile feeling when drinking a Coca-Cola in contrast to Pepsi's 54 percent.

A similar yet closer battle is taking place in Japan where the majority of drinks show up in glass bottles. Through our group sessions across the world we noticed that consumers in Spain, Poland, Britain, Denmark, South Africa, Germany, India, and Thailand were all able to describe precisely the tactile feeling of the glass Coke bottle. This unique touch point no longer exists in the United States. The irony of this is that this loss could have been so handily avoided. Unfortunately, this failure is likely to be repeated when Coke's bottle-replacement plan gears up in the international marketplace.

This is not only a cautionary tale about how Coca-Cola was once about to lose its tactile grip, but a story about how economic efficiencies in production and distribution have consistently downgraded the look, sound, and feel of the product. In addition to this, the difficulty of maintaining quality in the mix machines across the globe has further weakened the distinctive taste of the product. All this results in a consistently weaker brand across not three but all four senses. This downgrade is proving to be lethal to the brand.

The Sniff Test

Smell is a potent wizard that transports us across thousands of miles and all the years we have lived.

HELEN KELLER

The smell of a rose, a freshly cut lawn, mothballs, vinegar, peppermint, sawdust, clay, lavender, freshly baked cookies . . . our olfactory system is able to identify an endless list of smells that surround us daily. Scents evoke images, sensations, memories, and associations. Smells affect us substantially more than we're aware of. We underestimate just how large a role it plays in our well-being. Smell is also the oldest part of our brain. It's played a vital role in our human survival, alerting us to distant danger, like fire. Via their sense of smell, animals instinctively know to reproduce, find their prey, and avoid danger.

Smell can also alter our mood. Test results have showed a 40 percent improvement in our mood when we're exposed to a pleasant fragrance—particularly if the fragrance taps into a joyful memory.[13]

There are about 100,000 odors in the world—a thousand of them classified as primary odors, not to mention unnumbered combinations of multiple odors. Each primary odor has the potential to influence mood and behavior. Everyone perceives odor differently, since so many other factors come into play—including age, race, and gender, to name just a few variables.

Human beings' smell preferences have changed over time. In a study published in 1992 by the Smell and Taste Treatment and Research Foundation in Chicago, the neurologist Alan R. Hirsch asked nearly a thousand adult consumers at random to identify smells that brought on moments of nostalgia. What he discovered was that there was a divide between those born before 1930 and those born after. People born before 1930 cited natural smells—for example, pine, hay, horses, and meadows. Individuals born after 1930 were more likely to mention artificial smells like Play-Doh, marker pens, and baby powder. The year 1960 proved to be another watershed for the smell of freshly cut grass. Those born before that date liked it, while those born after associated it with the "unpleasant necessity of having to mow the lawn."[14]

In chapter 2 we established that practically everyone likes the way a new car smells, but what emerged in our Brand Sense study is that some cultures are more affected by aromas than others. A huge 86 percent of consumers in the United States find the smell of a new car appealing, whereas only 69 percent of Europeans feel the same way. Branding cars has moved beyond stylish design and powerful engines to make the car a multisensory experience.

Eau de Rolls-Royce

Hundreds of thousands of dollars were spent developing the distinct smell of the 1965 Rolls-Royce Silver Cloud. The smell is impossible to buy! Yet it's been an essential component in maintaining one of the world's primary luxury brands. I consider it a small masterpiece in sensory branding.

When Rolls-Royce started getting complaints about their new models not quite living up to their illustrious predecessors, they figured out that the only difference between the new models and their older ones—apart from the obvious—was the fragrance.

The interiors of older "Rollers" smelled of natural substances like wood, leather, Hessian, and wool. Modern safety regulations and building techniques mean that most of these materials are now obsolete, and have been replaced by foams and plastics. The only way that Rolls-Royce could recapture that essence was by artificially mimicking it. Using a 1965 Silver Cloud as a reference, the team began a detailed analysis of the aroma, identifying individual odors. They formulated a chemical blueprint for the essence of their analysis. In total, eight hundred separate elements were found. Some, like mahogany and leather, were expected, but others like oil, petrol, underseal, and felt were more surprising.

With this analysis in hand, Rolls-Royce proceeded to remanufacture the smell. Now, before each new Rolls-Royce leaves the factory, the unique smell of Rolls-Royce is added to the underside of the car's seats to recreate the smell of a classic "Roller." Cadillac has gone so far as to release its own signature scent. In celebration of the one hundredth anniversary of the car, Cadillac's new fragrance for men combines a mixture of grapefruit, chamomile, geranium, tarragon, and cinnamon, a fragrance intended to capture "life, liberty, and the pursuit"—rather than your grandfather tooling around town in a too-big car that gets ten miles per gallon.[15]

Essentially, this story illustrates the importance of maintaining perception—often without being aware of what the perception actually is.

Eau de Car

Cadillac works equally as hard as Rolls-Royce to ensure a loyal fan base. General Motors is making sure that nothing a potential buyer touches, hears, or smells is left to chance. Cadillac's new-car smell, that ethereal scent of factory freshness, is in fact a result of customized engineering. In 2003 the company introduced a special scent processed into Cadillacs' leather seats. The scent—semisweet, semisubliminal—was created in a lab, chosen by focus groups, and is now a part of every new Cadillac put on the road. It even has a name: Nuance.

For years the leather used in luxury cars was tanned, processed, and colored in order to neutralize its natural smell. It was then injected with industrial aromas. Today a process called "re-tanning" replaces fragrant oils into the leather. Research shows that our smell preferences have changed over the years. Believe it or not, we now prefer the smell of artificial leather to real leather—and car manufacturers are responding by going to great efforts to satisfy customer demands.

That takes branding to a whole new level! Ford, for example, has a specific branded aroma, which they've used since 2000. Like Ford,

Chrysler uses a single fragrance for all their cars. Other manufacturers use different scents for different models, a marketing strategy which bears fruit. According to the Brand Sense study, 27 percent of U.S. consumers believe Ford vehicles have a distinct smell, although only 22 percent can claim the same about Toyota. An even more dramatic trend occurs in Europe where 34 percent consider the Ford smell distinct—in contrast to only 23 percent who claim the same about Toyota.

Ever since Dr. H. A. Roth performed his simple yet powerful color-and-flavor tests in 1988, companies have been trying to develop tools to ensure a powerful connection between consumer perceptions and sensory realities. And the evidence is overwhelming. Take malls, for example. A study was carried out once in a suburban shopping mall to assess the impact of fragrance on consumer shopping. A citrus scent was periodically spritzed into the air—and consumers were duly interviewed as they left the store. The results showed that younger shoppers spent significantly more time in the mall during those times the ambient scent was sprayed.[16]

Many of the hotels in Starwood's Le Méridien hotel chain today exude a fragrance of old books and parchment. The scent machines are right in the lobby, though visible only to the most sharp-eyed guests. Their goal? To get visitors in a frame of mind aligned with the hotel's positioning as a destination for guests in search of new cultural perspectives and glimpses at history—even if they're situated in a super-modern hotel chain such as Le Méridien.[17] But that's just the beginning. In one UK airport, the aroma of baked chocolate chip cookies wafts through the baggage claim area. In London's Farnborough Airport, which typically hosts private jets and celebrity passengers, an enticing scent of green tea and lemongrass greets arriving guests. Toy manufacturer Hasbro has just introduced Smellaroos, which injects scents into children's board puzzles. There are even Yankee Candle–scented puzzles.

Still, little can compare to an event Polish concertgoers experienced during a 2008 production of the Artur Rubinstein Philharmonic Orchestra in Lodz. The entire building was suffused with the fragrance of roses. What's more, the fragrances changed according to what was taking place onstage, covering a range from heavenly and delicate during romantic moments to dry and nearly suffocating during times of peril or abandonment. The aim was to involve the audience in a completely sensual, utterly revolutionary way so that they could quite literally inhale what they were seeing.[18] This multisensory extravaganza coincided with the 2009 debut of French fragrance designer Christophe Laudamiel's "scent opera" at New York City's Guggenheim Museum—a piece of performance art five years in the making that conjoined music with an artfully orchestrated sequence of fragrance.[19]

But wait until you catch a whiff of what the future holds. A company called TriSenx has developed a product known as the Scent Dome, an addition to your home computer, which can release aromas online via the Internet. The Scent Dome stores an enormous variety of fragrances, which can be liberated via an electronic pulse mechanism. Imagine sending the man or woman of your dreams the aroma of freshly cut flowers, or chocolates. In conjunction with two leading companies (Firmenich and ScentSational Technologies), AquaScents has been set loose on the world—a line of bottled drinking water that gives consumers the experience of smelling fresh lemons or peaches when they unscrew the tops (without any calories or preservatives, either). ScentSational is also developing aroma release technology to inject fragrances into plastic packaging—which could someday include scented cup lids to enhance the cup of freshly brewed coffee you drink on your way to work.

Taste . . . and Smell

Smell and taste are in fact but a single composite sense, whose laboratory is the mouth and its chimney the nose . . .

JEAN-ANTHELEME BRILLAT-SAVARIN

Taste and smell, which are closely interlinked, are known as "the chemical senses," since both are able to sample the environment.

Many studies indicate that we often eat with our noses, which is another way of saying that if food passes the smell test, it will most likely pass the taste test. In our Brand Sense survey, when questioned about the smell and taste of McDonald's food, consumers tended to react positively to smell and taste, or negatively to both. They didn't hate the smell but love the food, or vice versa.

It is possible to take advantage of aroma without including taste. However taste without smell is virtually impossible. Taste is closely related to smell, but it's also closely related to color and shape. Look no further than the language of chefs who talk about retaining natural color and/or deep color. We consumers associate certain colors with certain tastes: red and orange are sweet; green and yellow are sour; while white tends to be salty.[20]

The use of taste to support products is by its very nature extremely limited. Despite this, there are still unexplored opportunities that could be exploited. Even the most obvious "taste" products—for example, in the dental care business—have so far failed to make use of this opportunity. As I asked earlier about Colgate, couldn't the smell and the taste of major toothpaste brands be extended to encompass dental floss, toothbrushes, and toothpicks? Currently the only synergy we see in this department is, with few exceptions, the use of the brand name and the corporate colors.

Apart from the obvious physical barriers that limit companies from taking advantage of taste, the late author Susan Sontag described the elusive nature of this sense: "Taste has no system and no proofs." Smell works over long distances, while taste quite simply doesn't. Our emotions can be triggered by a vague whiff of a long-ago fragrance. A mothball can conjure up warm and cuddly feelings for a grandparent; the smell of motor oil can take you back to when you were helping your dad fix the family car.

These bygone associations are referred to as the Proust phenomenon, and are named after Marcel Proust, the great French novelist famous for his memoirs in the early twentieth century. The Proust phenomenon is increasingly being triggered by branded smells. In older studies a large group (80 percent male and 90 percent female) reported having vivid, odor-evoked memories that trigger emotional responses. In 1987, *National Geographic* surveyed 1.5 million readers and questioned them about half a dozen odors. Gilbert and Wysocki reported on a subgroup of 26,000 within this same survey. Half of those who were forty years of age and over could connect a memory to at least one of the six odors. Memories were recalled in response to both pleasant and unpleasant odors, particularly if the odors were intense and familiar. Dr. Trygg Engen of Brown University conducted studies that contradict earlier findings about the predominance of vision, and concludes that our ability to recall scents and odors is much greater than our ability to recall what we have seen.[21]

Smell, touch, and taste are, of course, critically important in the language of love. To touch and taste another taps into our most elemental selves, and so our species continues. In fact it's been shown that extracts from male sweat can affect the regularity of a woman's menstrual cycle.

Pieter Aarts and J. Stephan Jellinek are psychologists who have studied how people's feelings, judgments, and behavior are subconsciously shaped by odor. They refer to this as the Implicit Odor Memory.[22] Their findings support the premise that fragrance is a decisive factor when a consumer buys, collects, or uses a product. We can therefore conclude that odor plays a very important role in consumers' acceptance of a brand. Increasingly aroma is becoming a highly effective brand "plus." Visual power has become dissipated in a world that bombards consumers with visuals all day and all night. There's so much visual clutter that people are becoming skilled at moving through it wearing "blinkers." Given this overexposure, attention to visual messages has naturally decreased.

Two identical pairs of Nike running shoes were placed in two separate, but identical rooms. One room was infused with a mixed floral scent. The other wasn't. Test subjects inspected the shoes in each room before answering a questionnaire. Overwhelmingly, consumers—by a startling margin of 84 percent—preferred the shoes displayed in the room with the fragrance. What's more, these consumers estimated the value of the "scented" shoes on average to be $10.33 higher than the pair in the unscented room.[23]

Another experiment was conducted in Harrah's, a casino in Las Vegas. One area was set aside and infused with a pleasant odor. Over the next few weekends, the revenue of the machines was compared to the earnings of the machines in the unscented zone. Revenues from the scented area were 45 percent higher than those from the scentless counterparts. Understandably, over the past few years Harrah's casino has spent thousands of dollars to see whether fresher air, wider aisles, and back supports can increase gambling—and today most casinos in Las Vegas including Bellagio, The Venetian, and Mandalay Bay have implemented similar strategies.

The Hilton in Las Vegas went so far as to release a scent manufactured by Alan Hirsch, a Chicago neurologist. The scent, known as Odorant 1, was placed in a slot machine pit, and the increase in revenue paralleled that in the Harrah's experiment.

The capacity of a brand to include aroma as part of a sensory experience naturally depends on what type of business it is. But whatever the line of business, a steady increase in branded smells is taking off as we speak.

Smell and the Supermarket

All around the world people and companies are becoming aware of the power of scent. Just like the movie theater owner I mentioned earlier, the average Disney World popcorn attendant has a wonderful working knowledge of how smell affects his business. He knows that when business slows down, all he has to do is turn on his artificial popcorn smell and in no time at all he has a line waiting for their popcorn. Woolworth's in Great Britain knows this, too. In a buildup to the holiday season, twenty of its stores introduced the smell of mulled wine and Christmas dinner. WH Smith, the largest newspaper/magazine chain in Europe, also went all out for Christmas and introduced the smell of pine needles.

Victoria's Secret has their own blend of potpourri, lending their lingerie an instantly recognizable scent. Superdrug used a chocolate odor in a Central London store on Valentine's Day. The London Underground filled some of its busier platforms with a refreshing perfumed scent called Madeline, hoping it would add a touch of cheer for the Tube's three million passengers, not to mention offering them a few moments' respite from some of their less hygienic fellow commuters.

Several chain stores are starting to introduce branded smells. Thomas Pink, also known as Pink, a British store that specializes in fine shirts, has introduced sensors in their stores that emit a smell of freshly laundered cotton to consumers. The response? Overwhelmingly positive.

The future of brands is not only about instilling new sensory appeals, but identifying the brand's existing sensory assets. Crayola is one of many companies that has begun seeking to trademark its most distinct smells, starting with their crayons, their primary product, which have no doubt left their odor imprint on the memories of millions of children who drew with them. Just ask those tweens from the *Today* show, who recognized the scent almost instantly!

The Swiss-based flavor and fragrance company Firmenich, one of the world's largest aroma and flavor companies, has sniffed the direction where brands are heading. Instead of following the normal aroma and flavor development processes, they have decided to let the brand become the centerpiece of its own development. The move indicates the beginning of a manufacturing trend in the flavor and fragrance industry. By turning the very scientist-driven development process upside down, the firm now ensures that the brand values will control the very signal that their products convey.

In the big picture, companies can take advantage of every single human sense to build a better, stronger, and more durable brand. The road ahead is not necessarily easy. Many challenges are around the corner. Sensory signatures that characterize any brand need to be identified, and it's vital that we as consumers feel comfortable with sensory brands. As I say, it won't be simple—but it's altogether possible, and the prospect is altogether exhilarating.

Highlights

To a large extent marketers have operated in a visual and auditory world, only occasionally venturing into a broader universe where they make use of all five senses. Increasingly consumers are expressing the desire for a complete sensory approach. Of the sample population we surveyed in our Brand Sense study, 37 percent listed sight as the most important sense when evaluating our environment. This was followed by 23 percent listing smell. Touch ranked lowest on the scale. More generally, the statistics show a very small differential when it came to a sense-by-sense evaluation, leading us to conclude that all five senses are extremely important in any form of communication and life experience.

Sound

Hearing is passive and listening is active. The sound of a brand should target both the hearer and the listener since each one is important in influencing purchase behavior. While hearing involves receiving auditory information through the ears, listening relies on the capacity to filter, selectively focus, remember, and respond to sound. Many elements of our everyday life are clearly associated with sounds. If we don't hear them, we miss them. The sound of a brand adds to the perception of product quality and function. If removed, the perception is diluted. It is extremely important to assess the role of product-generated sound because, increasingly, consumers are becoming more aware—and critical—of this phenomenon.

Sight

Vision has until recently been perceived as being the most powerful of our five senses; however research indicates that this may no longer be true. Whatever the case, there's no escaping the fact that distinctive design often goes hand in hand with distinctive brands, and successful brands are by their very nature visually smashable. Pharmaceutical companies make their tablets and capsules in all shapes, sizes, and colors, with each one intended to differentiate the product, impart a particular emotional "feel" to the drug and instill customer loyalty. The automobile industry is another category where shape plays a vital role. In many models, shape has become the defining feature.

Taste and smell

Closely interlinked, smell and taste are known as the chemical senses since both are able to sample the environment. Smells affect us substantially more than we're aware of. Test results have showed a 40 percent improvement in our mood when we're exposed to a pleasant fragrance—particularly if the fragrance taps into a happy memory.

CHAPTER 5

Being Alive

WHEN ONE OF THE WORLD'S LARGEST banks released its first-generation website, it took close to a full minute to open. Like many other banks, the NAB was known for long lines at the tellers. An independent survey was conducted asking visitors' general impressions of the new website. Even though there was no direct relationship between the long lines at the bank and the long download time of the website, consumers saw the website as just another delay conundrum caused by the bank. The survey elicited comments to the effect that the bank had managed to do in cyberspace what it already did in its branches—keep people waiting.

Consumers' perception of a brand is as good as reality. Whether the consumer compares the long waiting time on the Internet to long lines in the branches, or wine seems to taste better sealed with a cork, or a Rolls-Royce is perceived as riding more smoothly if it has a leathery smell, it's essential that a brand's sensory touch points be kept alive. These touch points should be maintained and enhanced since they're what give the brand its unique blueprint.

Discarding valuable sensory touch points will downgrade a brand.

Remember: a message is enhanced by appealing to several senses as it stands a far better chance of breaking through. The Brand Sense study confirms that the more positive the relationships established between our senses, the stronger the connection is between sender and receiver. Really—it's as simple as that.

A fabulous photograph of a freshly picked apple glistening with morning dew might entice you, but only in the most abstract way. But if a consumer could smell it, and hear it being sliced, it might convince him or her to buy a bagful of apples. Add to this picture a texture that might even give you a taste and you'd certainly be far more inclined to buy it. Ironic as it may seem today, this phenomenon seldom happens. I've studied literally thousands of TV commercials over the past couple of years, and I'd go so far as to say the exact opposite has taken place. Television ads for fast-food chains never let us hear the sizzle of cooking food, ads for soft-drink companies eliminate the clink of ice cubes, or the snap of the tab opening; ads for coffee seldom if ever let us hear the grains brewing, or the steam rising from the espresso maker. Why? Because the executives in charge believe that the contemporary TV viewer is 100 percent rational. There's no need, they believe, to play this or that theme song another time, whether it's a sizzle or a snap. I don't know about you, but even though I've done a great deal of work with fast-food and soft-drink companies, I still get cravings when I hear those sounds. And craving leads to desire . . . which leads to a sale. Like it or not, our senses are hardwired to seduce us—yet most brands believe that sensory stimulation is a thing of the past.

As I've said time and again, branding has always been about establishing emotional ties between the brand and the consumer. As in any relationship, emotions are based on data we gather from our five senses. Online dating agencies are one of the Internet's most successful financial operations. You begin with a photograph, move on to hearing a voice . . . and if both convey positive impressions, you may be persuaded actually to "talk to the photograph" at the other end of the telephone line. All the cues may be pointing in the right direction, but unless there's a physical presence you will never know if you even want a second date. All our senses are required to evaluate our choices fully.

Brands are no different. Up until now communication has been confined primarily to the visual and auditory model with an occasional scratch-and-sniff scent added to the random perfume ad. But brands shouldn't hesitate to venture into the worlds of taste, touch, and smell. Again, why? Because the very purpose of sensory branding is to ensure the integration of our five senses in all of our purchasing decisions.

Sense-Surround

Imagine this: You're strolling down a city street on a summer's day. The air is hot, the traffic's congested, the exhaust fumes are hovering, and there on the next block you see an ice-cream shop. As you get closer, a scent of fresh-baked ice cream cones wafts toward you. Without giving it any conscious thought, you find yourself drawn to the store or the street vendor. Ice cream strikes you as the perfect antidote to the heat and the traffic. Before you know it, you're continuing your journey with a cold, delicious ice-cream cone in hand.

Sensory branding™ aims to stimulate your relationship with the brand. You could say it sparks our interest, amps up our impulse purchasing behavior, and allows emotional response to dominate our rational thinking.

Two sets of stimuli can take place—branded and nonbranded. That ice-cream shop aroma could have belonged to any number of products. But a combination of aroma and the signage on the store helps create a brand association with a specific product. An association that, again, may arise unbidden the next time you're walking down the street in the heat. So what began as an unbranded experience is likely to morph into a branded one.

A branded stimulus not only motivates impulsive shopping behavior, it also directly connects emotions to the brand. Okay, let's imagine it's another sweltering day. You're sitting outside at a restaurant in front of a glass of ice with a piece of lemon, and hearing the sound of a drink whooshing open and being poured in the glass. Chances are you're thinking of Coke. Because 78 percent of those surveyed have positive associations with the bubbling sound of an opening Coke can—or bottle. The fact is that this distinctive sound of Coca-Cola has similar strong associations all across the world.

In Scandinavia, a home-delivery ice-cream company has taken the Pavlovian dog analogy I referred to earlier to another level. A small blue van drives up and down the neighborhood ringing a bell. After almost thirty years of riding around the neighborhood, 50 percent of the population associates the sound with ice cream—not just any ice cream, but more specifically with Hjem-Is ice cream. Once, as I was sitting in my rented car in the Philippines, I noticed that a sudden smile would appear on people's faces when they became aware of that sound—a smile, I might add, that was utterly missing when they viewed logos for local candy or soft drinks. The sound itself is owned by Nestlé—and the small blue-and-white bicycles that go around selling Nestlé's ice cream have been part of the scene in Manila for more than thirty years.

To achieve a branded stimulus is one of the hardest aspects of a sensory relationship to establish. It's not intuitive, and takes time to form. It requires constant reinforcement between a consumer's need and a specific brand. Branded stimuli create long-term loyalty. Nonbranded stimuli create impulsive, but nonbranded, behavior patterns.

Enhance

Just as a hologram allows us to see the same figure from different angles, so sensory branding allows consumers to see different dimensions of a single brand. Philippe Starck is a French designer who has turned his hand to everything from toilet-paper holders to hotel interiors, Puma shoes, and Microsoft's latest optical mouse. As diverse and even wacky as this range is, each item redefines the traditional appearance of good design while maintaining function. Starck designs bring a fresh vision to everyday items, forcing us to see them in a whole new way.

There are two levels on which enhancing brands operate—

branded and nonbranded. Toilet paper manufacturers are adding fresh-smelling scents enhancing impressions of sanitation and quality. This almost generic enhancement may affect the perceived quality of the product, but frankly, it does little for the brand. The most effective strategy therefore is to create a branded enhancement that, unlike a nonbranded one, reflects the brand, adds distinction, and differentiates it from all the others on the shelf.

Texas Instruments has developed an exclusive touch, specific to the keys on their calculators—a branded enhancement that makes the feel of a Texas Instruments calculator completely different from that of any other calculator. Similarly, Apple users are well acquainted with the Apple function key that replaces the generic "Ctrl" that's so familiar to PC users. The name is part of the function and becomes part of the thought processes of any Apple user. The action is both branded and intuitive, making it an ideal example of branded enhancement.

Bond

The ultimate goal in sensory branding is to create a strong, positive and long-lasting bond between brand and consumer so the customer will turn to the brand repeatedly while barely noticing competing products.

IBM ThinkPad notebooks have managed to create just such a bond. These laptop computers navigate with a TrackPoint mouse. The system has been trademarked by IBM, ensuring their competitors do not duplicate it. The result: IBM ThinkPad users remain loyal to the brand in that consumers who become accustomed to this system find it very difficult to switch to a touch-pad system of navigation.

Navigation is one of the most powerful ways for a brand to bond with the consumer. Whether it's an IBM TrackPoint mouse, a Nokia cell-phone menu, or Apple's icons and setup, once a navigation system has been mastered there is a natural resistance to relearn a whole new system. The process has become intuitive and most people are reluctant to interrupt their day-to-day flow.

Purpose of Sensory Branding

Emotional Engagement

Sensory branding offers the potential to create the most binding form of engagement between brand and consumer we've ever witnessed. The goal is to build a very loyal relationship over a long period of time. In order to establish this bond, the sensory appeal must have two essential ingredients: it has to be unique to the brand, as well as habitual. Not all sensory branding initiatives will necessarily be able to generate such high levels of loyalty, but if the brand maintains a distinct sensory appeal that is not imitated by any competing brands, loyal customers will follow.

Optimize the match between perception and reality

Before Carlsberg released its new plastic bottle, it was tested repeatedly. Danish focus groups were conspicuously aware of the change in the sound of the bottle opening. As a result of the company's findings, a special campaign was established to prepare customers for the change in sound and tactile feeling.

Too many brands allow too wide a gap between consumer perception and product reality. To narrow this gap, some flower shops add artificial fresh-flower odor to their stores. The genetic code of supermarket grapefruit has been tampered with to make the fruit easier to pack, which has transformed the taste. Consumers now expect their grapefruit juice to taste more like the supermarket variety. A juice company that grows its own grapefruits needs to be mindful of this "supermarket" flavor and figure out a way to get their juice to resemble it.

If quality is associated with substantial weight, then weight must be added. If the rolling down of the automatic car window doesn't

sound like "quality," the sound will have to be altered. In all cases, reality must shift closer to perception. The goal is for the reality to match, and if possible exceed, consumers' perceptions.

The Importance of Product Extensions

As each brand develops brand extensions (such as Marlboro coats and jackets), the links between the many products may erode unless a careful brand-extension strategy has been put in place. Consumers are able to make illogical leaps in product variety—for example Caterpillar tractors, and Caterpillar shoes. In the case of Caterpillar, as with Gillette, the brand value is "masculinity." This has been translated into the use of materials—rubber, metal, colors, and an overall toughness.

Trademark

The challenge brands will face in this new century will be their capacity to protect their identity from competitors. The best way to do this? Via sensory branding. Almost every aspect of a brand's sensory appeal can be trademarked. Trademark-able components are known in the industry as "trade dress." A trade dress is how a product smells, sounds, feels, tastes, and is shaped. Each component has to be distinct. Hey, I'm not saying it's easy! Harley Davidson once lost a court case in a fruitless attempt to guard their specific sound. In their case their sensory touch point belonged to a nonbranded type of engine, so legally at least, the company couldn't claim the sound as exclusively their own.

Sensory Translation

What makes a brand vastly more successful at a multisensory approach than another? In the majority of cases, these brands have achieved this with well-planned strategy executed over a long period of time—often decades.

We discussed a few of these brands in chapter 2—Singapore Airlines' Stefan Floridian Waters sprayed on hot towels and distributed to passengers, the distinct crunch of Kellogg's cornflakes, or the stylized Bang & Olufsen phone with its unique feel and sound.

Any company can build a sensory brand, which engages in a multisensory dialogue with its customers.

Case Study: Ferrari—Speeding Ahead Across the New Sensory Landscape

As champagne corks popped at the 2004 Grand Prix World Championship, another slightly different Ferrari model was about to leave the factory. The recognizable features of the legendary racing car were in place—the brilliant red finish, the prancing black horse—symbols which over six decades have become synonymous with innovation, speed, and sophistication.

The new Ferrari 3000 hadn't neglected the sound either. Experts also concurred that the 3000's speed paid homage to Ferrari's legendary status. To be sure, the Ferrari mystique was tangible on the day this new model was unveiled to the global press. There was, however, an additional buzz. This new Ferrari had no wheels and its engine was minuscule.

As you may have guessed, this new model wasn't a car at all, but a computer. Credit the car manufacturer's sensory appeal for creating the unlikely partnership of Ferrari and Acer, a computer manufacturer. Together they produced the Ferrari 3000, the world's first laptop fully clad in patented Ferrari-red. Although tenuous, even bizarre, at first glance, the link between the two highly divergent brands actually made sense. Acer had been an official supplier of electronic components to the Ferrari racing team for years. The same year, the popularity of the Ferrari laptop meant that the Italian-based Ferrari factory ran out of its trademark red paint. Why? It turns out the laptop was just too popular!

Ferrari and Acer. It's certainly an innovative brand alliance, but more than that, it's an intriguing combination of sensory touch points. Apart from the color, the notebook, like the car, has three coats of high-quality automotive paint, as well as a brushed silver interior. The finish and the feel of the computer duplicate the finish and the feel of the car.

The same sensory synergy remains consistent in all Ferrari electronic products. In celebration of Olympus's sponsorship of the Ferrari Scuderia Formula One Racing Team, the company released a Ferrari digital camera. Its body is Ferrari red, and it underwent five separate color checks in order to ensure accuracy. The aluminum parts are all hand polished. The Ferrari 2000 camera reflects the same fine lines of a Ferrari automobile. The high standards of both companies are combined in a limited edition, high-quality camera that comes in a suede case with a custom-designed strap.

The navigation for both the camera and the notebook is in sync with the design and navigation of the latest Ferrari car models. The notebook has also taken advantage of an additional touch point—namely, when you start it up, it revs like a race-car engine. It's a sound so powerful and distinct that consumers can't fail to recognize it, and it's brilliantly integrated into all Ferrari merchandise (you can hear it when you log on to the Ferrari website, too).

The Ferrari 3000 is a fine example not only of how brands can team up to take advantage of each other's sensory strengths, but of how differentiation in one of the most competitive markets can be secured by increasing sensory touch points previously neglected by the manufacturer.

By appealing to the tactile sense via the distinct Ferrari paint finish, and by leveraging the sound of speed, and the branded color, Acer and Ferrari have managed to differentiate their notebook from the standard generic and basic gray models that exist. And consumers turned out in droves.

Highlights

Project Brand Sense confirms that the more positive the synergy that's established between our senses, the stronger the connection made between sender and receiver. Discarding valuable sensory touch points downgrades a brand. A marketer's primary objective therefore should be to ensure that all the historical links and associations connected to the brand in question are supported. If marketers fail to do this, they are at risk of losing some of the strongest competitive advantages of your brand—and we as consumers will walk away.

CHAPTER 6

Moving Mountains

JANUARY 14, 2004 WAS A LANDMARK in the life of a teenager with the unlikely name of Will Andries Petrus Booye. He lay face-down on a table, where he submitted his neck to a plastic surgeon's laser. The doctor worked slowly, carefully obliterating the tattooed bar code with the letters G-U-C-C-I neatly etched underneath—and bit by bit, he removed the tattoo. The process may have been painful, but it also marked the end of Will's obsession with the Gucci brand, one that had become, in Will's words, "My one and only religion."

I first met Will in the late 1990s, when his Gucci tattoo was brand new. Back then, Will believed he'd formed a lifelong relationship with the brand. Well, "lifelong" turned out to be approximately five years. During that time, Gucci for Will became a "person" to whom he could relate, whom he admired, and who supported him twenty-four hours a day, even lending him a firmer identity. He spoke about Gucci as if the brand were a family member rather than an expensive fashion product. He could expound at length about the company's designs, colors, and textures, as well as the smell of the perfumed Gucci environment.

But by the time Will had the Gucci name and bar code removed from his neck, he sensed the brand was losing its grip. What he'd once perceived as the ultimate made-in-heaven brand seemed to be slipping. Will wasn't alone in his thinking. Gucci's lack of innovation and dated advertising campaigns suffered a final blow when Tom Ford, Gucci's head designer, decided to go his separate way. What's more, the military was beckoning Will, offering him an alternate sense of family and self-worth.

Will deftly summed up his experience with Gucci for me one day. The admiration he had for the brand was stronger, he said, than with any person he knew. Gucci was like his own private, personal companion. Whenever he entered a Gucci store, he quite literally felt he was in heaven. Everything about the store made him feel at home, and at ease, from the atmosphere of luxury to the store design to the music playing overhead. Moreover, the borrowed status of the brand made Will feel like an exclusive member of a distinct brand community. After he got his tattoo, he was constantly approached both by friends and strangers, making him feel like the center of the universe.

One day, though, Will awoke to find the magic gone. Overnight Gucci had become unexciting. All that was left was the tattoo, which he proceeded to get rid of.

If you think Will's story is an example of extreme brand-obsession, consider David Levine, Christof Koch, and Mark Tappert—three men who live thousands of miles apart. There's a fifteen-year gap in their ages; they also have totally different careers. David is a psychologist, Christof a professor of computation and neural systems, while Mark works as a graphic designer. Yet despite these disparate demographics they have one important thing in common. Tattooed on their right arms is an apple. Not just any old apple, either. One with a clean bite, a short stalk, and two leaves. The globally recognized symbol of Apple computers. (Apple, I might add, is probably the most frequently etched tattoo of all brand enthusiasts across the world.)

To permanently etch the apple logo into their skin is a sign of these three men's unwavering faith in the Apple brand. For them, Apple has become an addiction like the faith and loyalty someone feels to his or her favorite sports team, music group, or even religion.

Religious fervor is based primarily on faith and belief. For that matter, sports are, too. At the risk of sounding crass, these days it can be hard to divorce faith and belief from big business. According to a study carried out in 2008, the U.S. religious publishing and products market—which encompasses everything from bibles to incense, candles to psalm books—is worth $6 billion.[1] In contrast, video games accounted for another $21 billion, while $24.2 billion was generated from nonreligious book sales. No doubt this is in part a reflection of our anxious times. Wars, financial challenges, a changing labor market, more people, fewer jobs, escalating crime, and an increasing divorce rate—as these and other uncertainties fill our days, all of us feel an increasing need for stability, for permanent foundations that offer solid promises. For a large percentage of the world's population, religion fits the bill in a world that's changing at a near-incomprehensible pace. It offers lifelong guidance on how to live and provides a road map that extends far into the future, even ensuring security beyond death.

At first glance, branding and religion sound like an odd, incongruous combination. Yet on further examination, the relationship is far closer than we dare imagine.

Fact: Branding continuously strives to achieve authenticity and build a relationship with consumers that extends, as the expression goes, from cradle to grave. By its very longevity, religion presumes an authentic, loyal, lifelong relationship with its adherents. Brands attach labels to physical products or services, while religion represents intangibles—phenomena that are difficult to describe and impossible to show or prove.

David's, Christof's, and Mark's devotion to Apple is unique. At the same time, it poses a question: Why have so few brands managed to create a devotional fervor? Is it reasonable to think that marketers and businesses can learn valuable lessons from religion when they're launching new products?

Always True to You in My Fashion

The more loyalty a brand inspires, the greater the potential it has for long-term success. As in all matters connected with belief, companies can't weigh, predict, or purchase loyalty. Loyalty is the result of a wide range of factors (including trust), which over time generate the kind of allegiance every marketer aims for—customers who can't do without their Crest, their Gillette razors, their Apple computers, or their Harley-Davidsons.

Just as strong as loyalty are traditions. But even if some brands claim a strong loyal following, few if any can claim to be part of a tradition.

Still, when you think about it, every day we're surrounded by traditions of both the secular and sacred variety. We pop champagne corks and marvel at fireworks on New Year's Eve. Every year Hindu homes are lit up for two weeks to ward off dark spirits during Diwali. Florists typically run out of red roses on Valentine's Day, and once a year on the Day of Atonement, Jews fast to cleanse themselves of sin. (I might add that many of these traditions are accompanied by gift giving and special foods.) Here's an odd question: How many people in the world do you imagine brush their teeth in the shower? Answer: Forty percent. Whenever I speak at conferences around the world, I'll sometimes ask people in an audience of, say, one hundred people, "How many of you brush your teeth in the shower?" I swear to you that almost without exception, precisely forty men and women will raise their hands.

What's more, we're willing to pay the hiked-up prices for flowers on Valentine's Day, and we also find time in busy schedules to send out Christmas cards. Why? Because these annual rituals are woven into the fabric of our lives—even though many of our most cherished rituals don't stand up to rational scrutiny in the twenty-first century. We don't question it—we just do it, in part because traditions and ritual offer a sense of predictability and continuity, bind us to our communities, and generally make us feel more secure in our lives.

Whether dreamed up by clever marketers or evolved over centuries, traditional celebrations are centered on rituals. In addition, families often create their own private rituals. Whether we're served a special kind of cake on our birthdays or insist on getting married in Grandma's old wedding dress, we participate in these irrational customs because they give us a sense of belonging in an at-times unsettling, constantly changing world.

As I briefly discussed in chapter 5, each of us has our own set of daily rituals, too—some 250 of them a day, if you can believe it, based on a study I once carried out. Yours may include grabbing a double espresso from Starbucks every morning en route to work, and ending your day with an ice-cold Corona or half a tub of Ben & Jerry's ice cream. For many, movies just aren't movies without a Coke and popcorn. Have you noticed how these brands have snaked their way into our national vocabulary? In fact, they've taken their followers up a rung on the loyalty ladder to become part of tradition.

Just like religious traditions, branded traditions are often passed from one generation to the next. Some families, for instance, make yearly visits to Disneyland, or to an old summer house that's been passed down for generations. During the long month of Ramadan when Saudi Arabians fast all day, as much as 12 percent of the population washes down their evening meal with Sunkist, a concentrated juice product—which today has become part of a ceremonial ritual. Johnson's baby powder may be one of the most recognizable fragrances in the world, but in Papua New Guinea, the product is seldom if ever used on infants and their diaper rashes. It's used in mortuary rituals to cleanse the odor of a recently deceased man or woman, and also sprinkled onto mourners to signal that the mourning period is over.[2]

Superstitious Bonding

As we consumers climb the loyalty ladder towards brand heaven, few brands in the world have achieved what I like to call "superstitious branding"—meaning, like Apple or Harley-Davidson, they are perceived less as brands than as a way of life. (I call them "superstitious" because it's as if by using them, they can almost ward off calamity.)

Jack Nicholson won an Academy Award for his role of Melvin Udall in the 1997 film *As Good as It Gets.* He played a curmudgeonly man with an obsessive-compulsive disorder. Walking across the checkerboard floor tiles involved painstaking concentration as the character played by Nicholson ensured that he never stepped on the black squares, only the white. Audiences the world over chuckled (or squirmed) at this peccadillo, since some part of us recognized and identified with Nicholson's condition. We "touch wood" to prevent a horror we've spoken of becoming reality, as if doing so will somehow change the course of our lives. We avoid walking under ladders, and on Friday the thirteenth we remain slightly more vigilant. We all engage in some degree of superstition to make our world safer. Is this rational? Hardly. However, we fear the consequences if we abandon these practices—and thus superstition becomes tradition.

The Beatles' "Rocky Raccoon" checked into his room, only to find Gideon's Bible. Rocky is hardly alone. In hotel rooms from Liverpool to Lahore, from Sacramento to Sydney, guests will typically find a religious book—a Bible or a Koran, perhaps—tucked away in the bedside drawer. There's no law prescribing or demanding that motels and hotels do this, yet for over a century, travelers can rest easier knowing that spiritual sustenance is only a drawer away.

No brand has yet succeeded in achieving this high level of dependence or trust, nor should we expect it to, but religion does provide a role model in terms of offering wisdom, loyalty, myth, metaphor, depth of meaning, and pure significance. After all, we're entranced by the stories of the world's great religions, and captivated by their history, symbols, and messages. They touch us at a fundamental emotional level, one which precludes any rational discussion.

In contrast, branding has become an ever more rational science. Maybe it's time to take one step back?

There's no doubt: People all over the world are in search of emotional fulfillment. The world is in a scientific headlock. We focus on rational argument and measurable outcomes. Is it any surprise to find an increasing need for emotional connection? The steady, ongoing attraction to alternative religions has become a fact of life. In my book *BRANDchild*, tweens (eight-to-fourteen-year-olds) clearly wanted emotions to be included in their entertainment, their commercials, and their brands. In fact 76.6 percent of the tweens we interviewed in the United States said they wanted something to believe in. A further 83.3 percent of all urban tweens regarded "obeying rules" as one of the most important choices they made. This figure was constant across the board, regardless of what country the respondent was born and raised in. Given this intense need for emotional connection, it's not surprising that between 2002 and 2007, sales of mainstream religious and spiritual books to the general public grew by roughly 7 percent over sales for secular books.[3]

Obviously, the gap between the rational proposition of today's brands and the need for emotional products, services, and beliefs is growing. Religion properly meets this need. If for no other reason, and without equating the two or seeming overly exploitive, branding should take a few lessons from the world's great religions and aspire to build ever-stronger emotional ties with the general population.

You Are My Sunshine

Icons

The best-known icons in the world are religious, among them the cross, the crescent, the meditative Buddha, the om, the ankh, and the Star of David. Each one carries an enormous symbolic weight. Each represents a way of life, a belief system, and a community for millions, if not billions, of people. Despite countless graphic representations of icons that proliferate throughout the world and continue to be created, these icons are easily recognized by just about everybody. Apart from their straightforward message, we've also seen them morph into all kinds of permutations. They're set in pendants, on flags, in art, atop buildings, on T-shirts, and in print. They come in every material substance you can think of.

Royal families the world over are also represented by symbols or logos. For example, each and every member of the Royal Family in Denmark has his or her own monogram. When a new member enters the family, a new monogram is carefully created and designed to reflect his or her personality.

Iconic messages tend to be multilayered and ambiguous. Non-Buddhists have adopted the Buddha as a symbol of enlightenment, while decorative crosses have become fashion statements for styles as diverse as the wayward gypsy and the hard-core, studded-leather punk rocker. Religious icons are the equivalent of the marketer's ultimate branding logo, except that marketers are looking for long-standing tradition, as well as for instant and widespread recognition. Nor are most of them willing to wait several thousand years to get there!

Spreading the Word

Not that long ago, nautical maps of Europe contained legends that included churches and other places of worship. Sailors often could find their way by glimpsing steeples and spires before they happened upon a lighthouse, which made churches an important navigation tool.

Churches once held the monopoly on the choicest real estate, and they also tended to situate themselves on the highest ground, so their grand steeples and graceful, cross-enhanced spires dominated the visible horizon. No building was permitted to be built higher, ensuring that the local church would always occupy the site closest to heaven. Despite modernization, the City of Rome still abides by a law that states that no building can be higher than the dome of St. Peter's.

Christianity is not alone when it comes to ensuring maximum visibility for its places of worship. Mosques and minarets dominate the skyline in many Muslim cities, and on the ever-changing high-rise horizon of Bangkok in Thailand, the tall curved roofs of shining gold Buddhist temples are easy to spot.

So all over the world religious buildings aren't just visible, they're accessible from every direction. The whole town knows where they are. The fact is, they're central to the formation of community, providing a sense of belonging and a sharing of core values.

Follow the Leaders

If you visit Bangkok's Pariwas temple in Thailand you will find more than the usual Buddha. There, a fan of soccer star David Beckham has taken celebrity worship to a whole new level. A one-foot-high shimmering gold-leaf statue of Beckham takes its place at the feet of Buddha along with other less celebrated deities. Chan Theerapunyo, the temple's senior monk, has defended the addition, saying, "Football has become a religion and has millions of followers. So to be up to date, we have to open our minds and share the feelings of millions of people who admire Beckham."

FIGURE 6.1 The ultimate belief . . . for some. A sharp eye would notice that one of the fifty Buddhas at Pariwas Temple in Bangkok is slightly different. It's a Beckham Buddha—in gold.

That said, the adoration of David Beckham pales in comparison to a Japanese cartoon character called Hello Kitty. For over twenty-five years, this bulbous cat with no mouth has earned the Sanrio Corporation literally billions. A website called Praying for Hello Kitty gives an indication of the power and near-messianic fervor of this brand. It's hard to dispute the underlying religiosity of a message posted on the Praying for Hello Kitty website that includes the lines, "Hello Kitty is a white angel who does not know any dirty . . . Hello Kitty is the Saint Maria . . . Hello Kitty is the creature which the God made first . . . Hello Kittyist world will prosper more and more . . . Jesus Hello Kitty, Our Hello Kitty . . .[4]

Just as each one of the world's religions is built around strong charismatic leadership, these same qualities are reflected in our most successful "personality" brands. The David Beckhams, Bonos, and Madonnas of the world can claim a similar power with their legions of devoted followers. More traditional brands follow this same trend thanks to their own strong charismatic leaders. Think Richard Branson, Walt Disney, or Steve Jobs. Each name has become synonymous with the brand he has created. The founder is the brand, as well as the brand itself—whether it's Virgin, Disney, or Apple—and is one of the defining lights in its adherents' lives. A light, I might add, that can occasionally dim. Steve Jobs endured his moments in the wilderness when he was temporarily ousted from Apple. Martha Stewart, the doyenne of household brands, has experienced her own fall from grace.

At a Macromedia conference in San Francisco some years ago I sat beside an Apple devotee who was clutching a Newton, the PDA introduced by Apple in the mid-1990s that despite its conceptual genius, never managed to break through. To everyone's surprise, Steve Jobs appeared onstage. Dressed in his characteristically casual attire, he kicked off his speech by proclaiming that the Newton was dead—then dramatically threw one of the devices into a nearby Apple bin.

Some members of the audience intuitively applauded, others were screaming, and still others were in tears. After the person next to me spent some time furiously taking notes, he joined the fracas, threw his Newton on the floor and started to jump on it. For him

Apple was more than just an electronic manufacturer—it was, dare I say it, a religion.

In another example of a famous corporate marketing failure, in 1984 Coke decided to follow the results of a taste test after a survey of nearly 200,000 consumers and tweak the formula of its recipe. New Coke marked the first change to the secret recipe in ninety-nine years. When the taste change was announced in 1984, some panicked soda-lovers responded by stocking their basements with multiple cases of the original Coke.

The results were catastrophic. Many consumers were not only outraged, but they also felt that a small piece of Americana had been unceremoniously discarded. Calls flooded the 800-GET-COKE phone line, as well as Coca-Cola offices across the United States. By June 1985, the Coca-Cola Company was receiving 1,500 calls a day on its consumer hotline, compared with a typical day's four hundred or so.

What the survey's tests hadn't shown, of course, was the bond consumers had created with the Coca-Cola brand. In this quasi-religious relationship, consumers didn't want anyone, including the Coca-Cola Company, tampering with the brand they'd grown to worship and adore. Protest groups including the Society for the Preservation of the Real Thing, and Old Cola Drinkers of America (which claimed to have recruited 100,000 members in a drive to bring back "old" Coke) popped up around the country. Songs were written to honor the old taste. Protesters at a Coca-Cola event in downtown Atlanta in May 1985 carried signs proclaiming, "We want the real thing" and "Our children will never know refreshment."

The return of original formula Coca-Cola on July 11, 1985, signaled the close of seventy-nine days that revolutionized the soft-drink industry. The sheepish (and newly transformed) Coca-Cola Company today stands as testimony to the potency of brands that are more than just brands. Unbeknownst to the company, Coke had taken on the trappings of a mini-religion.

Divine Inspiration

Harley-Davidson, Apple, and Coca-Cola have all provoked reactions and actions from their customers that other brands can only dream about. These brands' adherents are more than just customers—somewhere along the line they've been converted into full-fledged believers. You might argue that in their devotion and headlong loyalty, a great deal of rational thinking is absent.

So, what does it take to elevate a brand beyond its traditional loyal base of consumers towards a bonding that resembles a religious relationship? The first step requires paying close attention to the Ten Rules of sensory branding. These are the fundamental components that underpin religion and can serve as the ultimate role model for branding:

1. A sense of belonging
2. A clear vision
3. Enemies
4. Evangelism
5. Grandeur
6. Storytelling
7. Sensory appeal
8. Rituals
9. Symbols
10. Mystery

A Sense of Belonging

Every religion fosters a binding sense of community. Within the bosom of this community belief can cement relationships among its members, creating powerful feelings of belonging. Living in the same neighborhood or sharing a common culture doesn't necessarily create this sense of union. No—there has to be a social glue that not only binds common goals and values, but celebrates and mourns the same events. As the congregation invests their time and resources in the community, it creates social capital that further enhances a sense of unity.

Music communities have existed for as long as there's been music. But since the Internet altered our landscape, they've become well-oiled information disseminators and are now emulated by companies who seek to get their particular artist across to the general public. If it works for music sales, it follows that brand clubs might serve this same role.

Let's revisit David Levine, the self-professed "Mac nut," a lecturer in psychology at the University of Illinois. Levine is the proud owner of a suede Apple jacket adorned with several of the original Macintosh icons. He paid $400 for the thing, but has yet to wear it outside of his home. In fact his household is its own Macworld, its local Apple Store. He owns ten of the machines. Recently he spent $4,000 on a dual-processor G4, and another $2,000 on a large flat-panel cinema display. "I don't need it," he told me. "I did it to support the Mac."

Like all Apple aficionados and collectors, Levine identifies powerfully with the brand's culture and identity. In his closet you can also find Apple-logo T-shirts and even suitcases whose nametags are adorned with the Apple brand. He acknowledges belonging to a Mac community and readily acknowledges the religious connotations of his Apple affiliation. He believes that Mac users have a common, atypical way of thinking and of doing things. "Some people say they are a Buddhist or a Catholic," he told me. "We say we're Mac users, which means we have similar values."

Establishing a sense of belonging is fundamental to growing a community. There are approximately two million online communities, although fewer than 0.1 percent of them relate specifically to brands (which may reflect the unfortunate fact that shockingly few brands place the consumer, as opposed to the brand itself, at the center of communication).

Among the largest branded communities in the world is Weight Watchers. More than two million members show up at roughly thirty thousand meetings a year across twenty-nine countries. For over forty years, by offering encouragement and advice, Weight Watchers has worked hard to connect its adherents through common weight-

loss goals and challenges. Along with Alcoholics Anonymous, Weight Watchers is one of the few brands founded on the concept of creating a sense of acceptance and belonging. The organization then takes its global community one step further by providing a workable strategy to slim down.

Another brand that fosters a potent sense of belonging is the construction toy, LEGO. There are some four thousand LEGO communities around the world, comprising every single age group. Thus, if you're a seventy-five-year-old grandfather who loves nothing more than to build with LEGO blocks in your spare time, no one in the LEGO community will look at you askance. A quick walkabout through the passionate LEGO community shows a diverse array of members, from mathematics professors to the unemployed.

Then there are the devoted Manchester United aficionados who comprise some ten thousand different communities, ranging from individual football fans to those who play on the team and have since become heroes in Japan.

Everyone, everywhere, feels the need to belong.

A Clear Vision

Christof Koch is one of the world's leading neuroscientists. Koch had his Apple tattoo done while he was on an archaeological dig in Israel.

So what exactly motivates supporters to etch the Apple logo onto their skin, or Harley-Davidson fanatics to fill their wardrobe with motorcycle apparel? Well, these two brands in particular reflect a strong sense of purpose. Their followers are more than devoted aficionados—they're positively evangelical in support of their chosen brand. Some brands, as I mentioned earlier, are represented in public by visible, daring, or determined leaders. Richard Branson of Virgin has made several well-publicized attempts to pilot the first solo flight around the world in an air balloon. Steve Jobs returned to an ailing Apple and in less than a year managed to turn around the company's fortunes (all for the grand salary of $1). This is the stuff that legends are made of. But daring stunts and headline-grabbing leaders won't succeed unless a brand's vision is focused on its consumers. Koch wholeheartedly identifies with Apple, which exhorts

TATTOO BRANDS	percent
Harley-Davidson	18.9
Disney	14.8
Coca-Cola	7.7
Google	6.6
Pepsi	6.1
Rolex	5.6
Nike	4.6
Adidas	3.1
Absolut Vodka	2.6
Nintendo	1.5

FIGURE 6.2 BRANDED TATTOOS How do you measure the ultimate brand loyalty? Perhaps by asking consumers what brand if any they would be prepared to tattoo into their arm. Interpret the somewhat surprising results by yourself.

its customers to "Think different" and aligns itself with such luminaries and rebels as Albert Einstein, John Lennon, and Mahatma Gandhi. At its core, the Apple brand is far more than its stunning, stylish technology—it's a philosophy and an unconventional identity that its users cling to.

A brand needs to set challenges, question them, then conquer those same challenges by turning itself into a hero—just as musicians, sports stars, and movie celebrities do. And at the root of every challenge there has to be a clear sense of purpose, which helps consumers identify exactly who they are in relation to the brand.

Enemies

When recalling the cola battles of the 1970s, a senior executive at the Coca-Cola Company remarked, "Going to work was like going to war." The challenge between Coca-Cola and Pepsi took on a global dimension that had slight echoes of religious conflicts that have existed for centuries. The Bible or the Koran? Protestants or Catholics?

Naturally, war—in all its dimensions—is what brand competition is all about. Among other things, war unites citizens of large, diverse nations by refocusing the population behind a single purpose, or goal. Teams and entire nations come together during the U.S. Super Bowl or soccer's World Cup. Whose side are you on, for example, in the Microsoft-Apple debate? Avis cannily made itself a player in the rental-car market by famous declaring itself Number Two, while at the same time proclaiming, "We try harder." Avis has used the same slogan for forty years, constantly assessing their status as Number Two—an interesting proposition considering our cultural preoccupation to be Number One.

Pierre Bourdieu, a French psychologist, once remarked, "A choice of brand is a clear statement of who you are not!" A visible enemy gives people an opportunity to show off their colors and align themselves with the team or player they most strongly identify with—who may in some cases be the underdog. In 1991, Linus Torvalds, a twenty-one-year-old student in Finland, developed a new computer-operating system he dubbed Linux. Linux, as everyone knows, has since become hugely popular and profitable. Research indicates that about a third of all Web servers in the world today are powered by Linux, which makes it the second-most used system beside the tall, ever-powerful Microsoft.[5] Linux also enjoys the distinction of being Microsoft's sole competitor that has, to date, successfully managed to compete with the software giant. Linux followers' passion for their brand is legendary, even zealous. Many a Linux fan will showcase a Linux tattoo, but you would be hard-pressed to find a Microsoft logo etched into anyone's flesh.

To become strong, a brand almost needs to be positioned in relation to another brand. Contrast and conflict build up an archetypal "us" versus "them" situation. Back in the 1980s, the American ice cream business was controlled by three multinational corporations. So when Pillsbury, the owner of Häagen-Dazs, attempted to limit the distribution of a small Vermont ice-cream company, Ben & Jerry's, the young ice-cream makers responded with their now famous "What's the Doughboy Afraid Of?" campaign, a campaign that proved so successful that their sales increased by 120 percent that year alone.

This David-and-Goliath scenario gained consumers' empathy and support and helped place Ben & Jerry's ice cream firmly on permarket shelf. Over the next decade Ben & Jerry's grew to become one of the biggest players in the U.S. ice cream market, which ultimately culminated in the Anglo-Dutch corporation, Unilever, taking over Ben & Jerry's in April 2000, ending a twenty-two-year battle for the consumers' hearts and minds. David had *become* Goliath. The fight was over.

Ironically, few companies take advantage of this technique. Most opt to pretend that their competitors don't exist. But as in any top game, movie, sports event, or political campaign, it's the tension of a rivalry that generates excitement and involvement, creates fans and enemies, and ignites passion, energy, opinion, and argument. That's more than one can hope for when building a brand.

Evangelism

Evangelism is an essential component of any religion's history, anecdote, and mythology, and religious fervor rarely exists without a large dose of it. The world's major religions have established their credentials over the long course of time—often thousands of years.

But what is evangelism? It's spreading the word from one consumer to another, constituent to constituent, either by word of mouth, generational legacies, or any other way to get other consumers within "the fold."

Manchester United is a UK soccer club that has adherents in spades. Almost any one of its 53 million supporters can recite its story. After the Second World War, the club found itself bankrupt. Matt Busby was brought in as manager, and in less than a decade he miraculously turned the team's fortunes around. By 1956 Manchester United had qualified to enter European competition and even reached the semifinals of the European Cup. A year later Manchester United brought home the league title. But in the winter of 1958, the team traveled to Belgrade to compete against Red Star. On the journey home, the team plane stopped to refuel in Munich. It was snowing heavily that day, and the runway was icy. After two aborted takeoffs, the plane overshot the runway and its wings clipped a house. The crash resulted in the deaths of twenty-three people. Eight were from Manchester United's young team, known as "Busby's Babes."

The club's resilience, perseverance, and ability to overcome this tragedy have gone a long way toward creating the strength of the Manchester United brand, which earned $233 million in 2002. Ironically, even though Manchester United hasn't been the world's best-performing team, their supporters have remained ardent and steadfast, and their fan base continues to swell.

History adds a necessary credibility to brands. It also supports a product's, or company's authenticity, which is one of the reasons why a brand's background and the stories swirling around it are so important. The tragedy and eventual rebuilding of the Manchester United team adds an essential authenticity to the brand. The question then becomes, how do you succeed in creating authenticity if your brand lacks a back-story?

Tim Hortons, the Canadian chain, found a way around the authenticity problem for their new coffee outlets by basing their advertising campaign on customer testimonials that proclaimed it a "meeting place—a home away from home." Tim Hortons also emphasized the distinct Canadian-ness of its homemade baked goods. The brand also managed to generate myth by using one of its key symbols—a simple coffee mug. As the story goes, a Canadian who traveled halfway around the world was approached by two fellow Canadians who recognized him as a fellow countryman on the basis of his Tim Hortons mug—and a lifelong friendship ensued.

Grandeur

Imagine being the first man ever to climb Mount Everest. Do we remember the second man or woman who scaled Everest? I don't know about you, but I don't. Now imagine visiting a church, or maybe even the Vatican itself. When we visit a place of worship, among the vaulted ceilings and rich furnishings—frescoes, tapestries—we leave feeling humbled, awed, dwarfed. Picture the Temple of the Golden Buddha in Bangkok, with its nearly eleven-foot-tall Buddha, or more prosaically, some of the world's most iconic hotels, which are deliberately designed to evoke both wonderment and a sense of awe at man's ingenuity and capacity for risk taking, whether it's Las Vegas's Bellagio Hotel or Dubai's jaw-dropping Hotel Burj Al Arab—all of which are deliberately marketed to inspire feelings of grandeur.

Companies would be well-advised to focus their attention on the awe-inspiring factors that connect consumers to their brands. As the digital gadget market explodes, consumers are overwhelmed by instruction manuals and technical details. But when the Apple iPhone hit the stores, didn't it achieve almost overnight a sense of almost unprecedented grandeur? And where was its instruction manual? You could access it in a short online film.

StoryTelling

The New Testament. The Torah. The Koran. Every single religion in history is packed not just with history but with countless stories, some miraculous, some gruesome, some both. The most powerful, successful brands have stories attached to them as well—whether it's Disney's cast of cartoon characters (Mickey Mouse, Peter Pan, and Captain Jack Sparrow, among others) or the handwritten stories of a food's provenance that Whole Foods plants in front of their organic produce. Consumers are entranced by stories (particularly ones they can complete with their own imaginary endings, or meanings), and consequently line up in droves.

Hello Kitty, as I alluded to earlier, offers up such a story. The demand for the Japanese cartoon character in Asia is insatiable, and is steadily growing in the U.S. and European markets. Recently, in Hong Kong alone, 4.5 million Hello Kitties sold out in a short five weeks. In Taiwan, the local Makoto Bank launched Hello Kitty credit cards, cash cards, and account books—and watched as the bank's annual revenue skyrocketed.

Hello Kitty has a savior-like ability to entice people into her perfect world by offering stability and happiness. What could be more attractive to a consumer than a chaos-free universe where a constituent simply follows the rules—leaving it up to Hello Kitty to take care of you? Hello Kitty has twenty-five years' experience doing just that.

Her devotees are free to project their emotions onto her bizarrely endearing image. She has help lines, prayer sites, and private Hello Kitty counseling sessions.

Hello Kitty will also take care of your every material need. There are Hello Kitty tea sets, toasters, phone holders, backpacks, calendars, diaries, mouse pads, clothing, toys, motorcycles, erasers, valances, sheets, curtains, and bedspreads. Itochu Housing is selling a Hello Kitty–themed condominium to celebrate the cat's twenty-fifth birthday. Daihatsu Motor Company has produced a Hello Kitty car, complete with Kitty door locks, upholstery, and driver's console. As you might have guessed by now, this Japanese brand icon is a multibillion-dollar global business powerhouse. Sanrio, the company who gave birth to her, is one of the world's most successful purveyors of character-related kitsch, with roughly 3,500 stores in over thirty countries, to which they add about six hundred new products a month to the 20,000 or so products already available.

Hello Kitty is by no means the only symbol of a so-called perfect world. Another Japanese concept has shown enormous potential, namely, EverQuest, an online game operated by the Sony Corporation, which today has close to 3 million paid subscribers. When members were asked where they'd prefer to live—Earth or in Norath (the cyberplanet in EverQuest)—20 percent opted for Norath![6] In the same way religion holds out the promise of a perfect life, Norath is clearly a very attractive alternative to our own world. And EverQuest is hardly the only perfect universe in cyberspace. As I write this, there are more than twenty thousand online gaming communities comprised of more than 35 million people.

Both EverQuest and Hello Kitty are extreme examples of perfect-world icons. However bizarre it may sound, they offer a partial strategic road map for creating a "perfect"-branded world. The key to success in these concepts has been these brands' ability to create a set of unbreakable rules that offer consumers safety, not to mention the freedom to reinvent themselves in a world that's more controllable, and in the end, more comprehensible.

Sensory Appeal

No brand in existence can lay claim to appealing to all five human senses. Yet almost every religion can. Each denomination has its colors, its dress code, its icons, and its settings.

In Turkey, the Church of Hagia Sophia (Holy Wisdom) was built on the highest hill in Istanbul. Two men worked to create this astounding Byzantine structure, neither of whom had ever turned his hand to architecture before. The church they eventually created was constructed around a dome designed to entice the eye upward around the building, moving closer and closer to its center, and at last, resting on the altar.

Religious buildings traditionally impart a sense of awe, but they're also designed to convey a religion's values. As well as physical manifestations of the heavenly, these sacred spaces are imbued with evocative smells. Burning incense during the liturgy dates back to ancient Hebrew worship, and is recorded in Psalm 121: "Let my prayer be set forth in Thy sight as the incense." As this verse suggests, incense symbolizes the word of the prayer rising up to God. The Bible equates incense with visions of the Divine, most notably in the Book of Isaiah and the Revelation of St. John, while the smoke itself is associated with purification and sanctification.

Incense is by no means the sole province of Christianity. The earliest use of aromatic oils and herbs has been documented in ancient China, and they were also used in sacrificial religious ceremonies across ancient Egypt, Greece, and Rome. Oils and herbs also play an integral part of all the major religions in Asia, and are used in shrines, during prayer and meditation, as well as to ward off demons and evil spirits.

Perfume began its life as a magico-religious symbol of transformation once confined to sacred ritual. From there, it developed rapidly into something far more profane as the secret spread from the priests to the general population. In tantric ritual, for example, sandalwood oil is applied to a man's forehead, chest, underarms, navel, and groin. A woman is similarly anointed with jasmine on her hands, patchouli at her neck, amber at her breast, musk in her groin, and saffron on her feet. A wonderfully heady mix of spiritual deliverance and pure olfactory delight.

Religious buildings are also designed to carry sound. Whether it's the organ, the choir, ringing bells, gospel music, or the sound of chanting mantras, the resonant acoustics are an important characteristic of all houses of worship. Each religion has its own signature sound, specific sacraments, symbols, and rituals. The music that accompanies it is a vital part of worship—and of the very atmosphere.

It's difficult to "feel" or "touch" the soul. Therefore, each religion has devised a symbolic tactile reference, whether it's a wafer, a vermilion tikka on the forehead marked with a firm thumb, worry beads clenched within a palm, even the texture of sacred books.

In contrast to religion, brands have long struggled to convey complete sensory appeal—largely because brands tend to narrow their focus, concentrating only on the senses related to the primary function of the product.

Harley-Davidson is one of the few exceptions. The sound of their V-twin engine has become synonymous with their brand. In 1996 the company took Yamaha and Honda to court to defend its trademark sound, described by Harley's trademark attorney, Joseph Bonk, as "very fast, 'potato-potato-potato.' " Although the sound of a Hog (an affectionate term used by Harley aficionados) firing up may not be eligible for trademark protection, it's as emotional for Harley devotees as the first swelling chords of the organ that precede morning mass are to devout Catholics.

Rituals

Every four years a torch is lit at Olympia in Greece, then hand-carried by athletes (and celebrities) from different competing nations to wherever the Olympic Games are being held. This ritual is an integral part of the Games' opening ceremony, and continues to burn throughout the Olympics, before it's finally extinguished at the closing ceremony.

The ritual of the Olympic flame has always seemed to be nothing short of religious. According to the Associated Press, more people witnessed the ceremonial opening of the 2008 Beijing Games—the biggest audience ever for an Olympic opening ceremony not held in the United States—than have ever attended any given religious ceremony. That wasn't the only ritual, though. Next came the unfurling of the flags, the soaring music, the contests themselves and the award ceremonies. All of which followed strict guidelines that have evolved over the years and today are familiar to billions across the globe.

Everyone watches the Olympics, and why not? There's drama, excitement, tragedy, and tears. Even after the flame is extinguished, symbols from the rituals endure. In any former Olympic City, you'll notice signs that direct you to the Olympic Avenue, the Olympic Square, and the Olympic Arena. Brands would pay *millions* for such naming placement!

Brands need rituals, although very few have managed to create them. In the heady days of rock and roll during the 1960s, the Who's Pete Townshend accidentally smashed his guitar on the ceiling of a small club. The crowd's frenzied cheers goaded him along, so Pete Townshend smashing his guitar became a ritual at every single Who performance—a ritual that was subsequently adopted by another icon of the 1960s, Jimi Hendrix.

Interestingly, some of the most sophisticated brands with an abundance of rituals are relatively new, and all tend to be part of larger branded communities. Nintendo, Xbox, and Playstation all have rituals in common. Serious gamers will tell you that they adhere to strict rituals set by the gaming community which encompass everything from play patterns to cheat codes.

If a brand wants to transform its traditional consumer base into a community of believers, it needs to have rituals that embody principles of consistency, reward, and shared experience. Why? Because consistency satisfies customer expectations, helps spread the word, encompasses every aspect from navigation to announcement to purpose and also appeals to our senses. Rituals should also carry with them a built-in reward system. I don't mean any kind of financial gain. I'm simply talking about an experience that's pleasurable enough to repeat—over and over again.

The most important element? A brand has to ensure that whatever ritual it comes up with is a shared one. Rituals by themselves carry little weight. Sure, it's nice gazing at a beautiful sunset, but the vista only really comes alive if you can share it with another person. Better still, if a whole community witnesses that sunset together, it turns into a sacred moment—a reward almost.

Over the centuries religion has managed to turn ritual into a finely tuned art. Future brands need to include rituals as part of their package, though this is achieved only with difficulty. Still, it's well worth the effort.

Symbols

The entire structure of our modern world is based on symbols—a phenomenon that's far from new. The Christian fish, or icthus, for example, is a symbol that's evolved over centuries and centuries. Originally a secret code etched with a sandal in the sand by persecuted believers, today holographic replicas adorn station wagons loudly proclaiming the drivers' Christianity to the world at large. Almost without exception, religions have uncovered symbols to represent and identify their faith—whether they're scratched in a cave, carved on a rock, or adorned with precious jewels.

And iconographic communication is on the rise. Almost all computer games function around icons, which serve two distinct purposes—to impart information in a quick, simple, and understandable language, and to be used as code, recognizable only by the initiated (which in turn forms its own code, further endorsing a sense of belonging among its adherents, those chosen few). My earlier *BRANDchild* study revealed that 12 percent of tweens preferred written communication to verbal—while an astonishing 70 percent abbreviated their language on purpose while texting or chatting. As a result, tweens' written language has almost become expedient, and has made room for abbreviations, icons, numbers, and nonstandard grammar.

Gangs wear their colors, motorcycle clubs their insignias, while the under-eighteen set focuses on hair color, style, and fashion. We dress, walk, and talk in a manner that shows where our affiliations lie.

Having said this, only a small number of brands have consistently (but more often inconsistently) integrated symbols into their overall brand communication. Over the past decade, more than once both Microsoft and Motorola have altered the appearance of some of their best-known icons, including menu settings, icons, recycle bins, and so on. Car brands are also guilty of discarding their symbols—a huge mistake, since symbols reflect a brand's core values, and ideally should be so distinct that they're instantly recognizable to every customer.

Mystery

What are we here for? What happens when we die? Is there life on other planets? What does God look like? Of course, there aren't definitive answers. But that doesn't mean we're not obsessed with finding a solution!

The unknown factors in a brand have shown to be just as inspiring as those that are known. It's been said (or deliberately leaked) that only two chemists within the Coca-Cola Company know the drink's top-secret formula at any given time. As the story, or rumor, goes, in the entire history of the company only eight people in total have known it, and only two of them are still alive. The Secret Formula refers to an ingredient called 7X, a mixture of fruit, oils, and spices that gives the syrup its distinctive "Coke" taste. When, in 1977, the Indian government demanded the company reveal the formula, Coke replied that it would rather forgo the gigantic Indian market than reveal its secret formula.

How many people have access to the Colonel's recipe for fried chicken—better known as KFC? I have no idea—but the point is a brand's history often helps generate a mystique that attracts an audience. No one really knows if the secret KFC recipe was really, truly uncovered when the Colonel died, and his house was sold (when the new owner attempted to sell the "secret" recipe he claimed he'd found, everyone believed him).

The more mystique a brand can cultivate, the stronger foundation it has for becoming a sought-after and admired product. Religions have been cultivating mystique since their inception. However, only a few brands have learned from the experience and made good use of this tenth rule.

Highlights

As anxiety and uncertainty fill our days, there's an increasing need for stability. Consumers tend to invest time and money in things (and institutions) they believe will survive.

For an enormous percentage of people, religion provides certainty in a world that's changing at an incomprehensible pace. It offers a blueprint of how to live, and a road map that extends way into the future, going so far as to ensure security beyond death.

Branding continuously strives to achieve authenticity and build a relationship with consumers that extends from cradle to grave. By its very longevity, religion automatically assumes an authentic, loyal, lifelong relationship with its adherents.

Can religion be a source of inspiration for branding in the future? Brands like Apple, Harley-Davidson, and Hello Kitty have already become quasi-religions for most of their adherents.

In order to elevate a brand beyond its traditional loyal base of consumers towards a bonding that resembles a religious relationship, remember the Ten Rules (and consumers, be aware of them, too):

1. A sense of belonging

Every religion fosters a binding sense of community. Within the bosom of this community, belief can grow and cement relationships among members of the congregation, creating powerful feelings of belonging.

2. A clear vision

The brand needs to reflect a transparent purpose and should be represented by a visible, daring, determined, or charismatic leader.

3. Enemies

A visible enemy gives people an opportunity to show their colors and align themselves with the team or player that they most strongly identify with (including the underdog).

4. Evangelism

Evangelism is an essential component of any religion's history and mythology—just as it should be for any successful brand that hopes to attract new legions of consumers.

5. Grandeur

Religions and brands that imbue consumers with a sense of wonder and awe will connect us all indelibly to them.

6. Storytelling

Brands need to first create, then establish, a product that tells a story to which consumers can then add their own ideas and endings.

7. Sensory Appeal

No brand in existence can lay claim to appealing to all five senses. Yet almost every religion can. Each denomination has its colors, its uniforms, its icons, and its locales—just as a winning brand should.

8. Rituals

If a brand wants to transform its traditional consumer loyalty to a community of believers, it needs to have rituals. Traditional celebrations—whether thought up by clever marketers or evolved over centuries—always center on rituals.

9. Symbols

Iconographic communication is growing fast. All religions—and many present-day computer games—function around icons. Only a limited number of brands have consistently integrated symbols into their overall brand communication.

10. Mystery

Unknown factors in a brand have shown to be just as inspiring as the known. The more mystique and *je ne sais quoi* a brand can cultivate, the stronger foundation it has for becoming a sought-after and admired product.

CHAPTER 7

The Future

LIKE EVERYTHING ELSE, BRANDING IS EVOLVING. Over the next decade the dialogue within my industry will shift from better print campaigns and more catchy television commercials towards a whole new path. This much I know: Brands will have to stand out, beat their chests, assert uniqueness, and establish their identities as never before. Sure—traditional advertising channels will continue to hold sway, but they'll have to exist alongside other, nontraditional channels, which are mushrooming as fast as technology allows. Airwaves and cyber-highways are gridlocked with so many messages that sometimes it's hard to find a voice in the jam.

Fifty years ago David Ogilvy, Bill Bernbach, and Stan Rapp transformed how most of the world perceived advertising. Recently, though, we've undergone a digital revolution. We have more channels than we can change, and more websites than we can browse. We have mobile phones, PDAs and Skype, the Internet, and electronic games, CDs, and DVDs. We have phones that snap photos, and animated images at our fingertips. We can interact with machines and people across the world in real time.

What we're witnessing is the emergence of the interactive consumer. By now an entire generation (or two) has grown up with mouse in hand and using a computer screen as their window to the world. They respond to, even demand, shorter, snappier, quicker, and more direct communications.

A Few Predictions . . .

Over the next decade, sensory branding will be adopted by three categories of industry.

1. **The sensory pioneers.** Automobile manufacturers and pharmaceutical companies will lead the way in sensory focus and innovation over the next decade.
2. **The sensory adopters.** Telecommunications and computer industries are both fighting for definition and differentiation. After all, who can tell them all apart? They're most likely to look to the automobile and entertainment sectors for inspiration.
3. **The sensory followers.** A broad variety of industries including retail and entertainment are more likely to trail than to lead.

What does it take to move into the world of sensory branding? Each and every industry has the potential to adopt a sensory branding platform. Right now, some are way ahead, while others are way behind.

Sensory Pioneers

The Pharmaceutical Industry

Drug companies have a limited number of years of patent protection on their products. After that, those patents are game for anyone to copy, and they *are* being copied. A steady stream of generic drugs is emerging out of Asia. What's more, tighter restrictions are being placed on pharmaceutical promotions. Marketing departments may find that sensory branding provides the base they've been looking for to create a brand new platform—and a new shot of loyalty from their consumers.

Taking advantage of consumer loyalty by means of the tactile feeling of its products, packaging, colors, package design, as well as the brand's distinct sound, aroma, and flavor can provide a pharmaceutical company with a whole new arsenal for bonding with customers. Regulations in some countries challenge traditional trademarks on the shape and color of medication, but so far, no government has rejected a trademark on smell or taste. That opens up a welcome vista for companies that can count on a lifetime trademark, instead of a patent with a set expiration date.

The Automobile Industry

Sometimes it's hard for leaders of the pack to stay ahead of the pack. The car industry is now moving into the final phase of innovative sensory branding. They're working on a host of new sounds for seat adjustments, gearboxes, rails, indicators, hazard warnings, horns, and electric windows as well as designing a low-noise, branded-sound car cabin.

Today, every possible component of a car that represents a sensory touch point is being scrutinized, evaluated, and branded. Soon, every car brand will have its own branded smell, a branded tactile feeling, as well as its own distinct sound. It won't be long before each component will be trademarked as "exclusive" to the car model and brand. After which the manufacturer can take its trademarked components to market and extend them across . . . well, Route 66 and beyond. Porsche already has a diverse variety of products on the market. If you want, you can buy anything from Porsche umbrellas to Porsche glasses. These sensory touch points become the primary point of contact and connection—which goes a long way towards explaining why people who are Porsche aficionados are prepared to pay up to 40 percent more for a Porsche laptop than for any other brand.

Sensory Adopters

The Telecommunications Industry

The global struggle for telecommunication dominance is reminiscent of the car manufacturers' struggle in the mid-twentieth century. Again, Asia has taken a back seat to Europe and the United States in terms of innovation, this time in the cell phone industry. Then again, Asian manufacturers are poised to bring high-standard multisensory perspectives to their new offerings.

Every aspect of the mobile phone, from the tactile qualities, design, and display to the branded sounds that hiss and beep when consumers use the phones, down to the smell of the product, will be evaluated, enhanced, and improved over the next few years. An example is Immersion, a company whose technology allows you to "touch" someone over the phone. According to BBC online, "The company has been talking to mobile manufacturers to build in touch into future phones."[1]

The Computer Industry

Computers have borrowed the term "Sound Quality" from the automobile industry. This marks only the beginning of the race to gain the competitive advantage in every aspect but the size of the microprocessor.

Apple and Bang & Olufsen are providing the inspiration for a computer industry that's only recently become preoccupied with style and design. It's about time, too! Computers are also focusing on sound. Next up are the tactile elements, followed by the smell of the equipment (I happen to love the smell of a new computer). In the same way it's become standard to take advantage of that "new car" smell, computer brands will shortly be coming up with their very own versions.

In contrast to countless other industries, technological innovations are already built in to the product. Soon computers will be manufactured with a capacity to handle sensory channels (remember those fragrant emails I told you about earlier?). Since 400 million people around the world switch on a computer each day, computer engineers are focusing on the mouse to potentially house the multisensory "brain." Sony Corporation is working on it as we speak.[2] There, a team of experts, including a psychologist, is developing a mouse that will make the user "feel" what it's pointing to on the computer screen. The mouse could be installed on any Windows-based computer, and could deliver images, text, and animation directly to a user's fingertips. Although engineers are designing this technology primarily for visually impaired people, the potential for other applications—namely sensory branding—is enormous.

Sensory Followers

The Food Industry

However we feel about tampering with the genetics of what we eat, you'll be reading a lot about "food design" in the next decade. Sure—taste will always be important, but the Brand Sense results show that smell and appearance rank equally strongly on consumers' scale of importance.

The food industry is unlikely to leave things as they are today. They will persist in designing the smell of the product and the sound of the packaging, as well as controlling the sound your food makes when you eat it. They will tamper with the color and the flavor, creating new levels of sensory preference. Tweens will like their ketchup green and their Sprite turquoise.

In our contemporary urban society we're more familiar with picking apples from supermarket shelves than from trees. Few among us would ever be able to identify an apple leaf. Although most consumers savor the aroma of what they believe is real leather, a generation ago they were introduced to a fake leather smell that they now take as the real thing. The altered, artificial world appears more authentic than the real world! Technology has enabled companies like Nestlé, Coca-Cola, and Carlsberg to add aroma to packaging on the supermarket shelf. The issue of authenticity will determine how far this industry can go before it runs into a consumer backlash.

The Fast-Moving Consumer Goods Industry

The fast-moving consumer goods industry (or FMCG for short) category includes everything from toilet brushes to pens. Some industries within this category will be able to navigate the sensory path more handily than others. Through the work of designers like Terence Conran and Philippe Starck, everyday items have become increasingly visually sophisticated. The next step? Distinguishing your scent and sound from the other guy's. To survive in this new sensory-defined landscape companies will have to take their cue from more advanced industries and try to maintain a lead in their own.

The Travel and Hospitality Industry

Up until the close of the twentieth century, the hospitality industry was one of the most innovative leaders in the sensory branding department. But financial crises, SARS, terrorism, swine flu, a tattered economy, and a general wariness about travel have been stalling their lead.

Only a few hotel chains—like the Ritz-Carlton—are maintaining their sensory focus. The Ritz's lion logo can be found on door handles, cake towers, soaps, and slippers. Yet despite the general loss of focus, the chains will remain innovators, with the Asian groups—particularly the Singaporean ones—at the forefront.

The travel industry has taken a hit all around. Budget airlines have forced regular airlines to cut their branding budgets down to nothing. Despite various crises, a few airline companies—Cathay Pacific, Singapore Airlines—have managed to keep their sensory touch points alive. Interestingly, these two companies have shown the clearest signs of recovery, which places them in a highly exclusive league of profitable airlines.

The Financial Institutions

As banks merge and grow, the consumer becomes increasingly insignificant, creating an ever-widening gap between institution and, well, you and me. Only a human touch can reestablish the bond, and sensory branding will create one of the connections.

As everyone knows, the banking retail environment has become increasingly automated. Costs have been passed on to consumers, who prefer dealing face-to-face rather than conducting their transactions through ATMs, the telephone, automated websites, and voice machines. In stark contrast, other retail businesses have chosen the opposite strategy, creating cozier, friendlier, lighter, more welcoming and, well, better *branded* environments.

Financial institutions now deal in commodity products. The days of a friendly manager with a reassuring smile and a warm handshake are fast disappearing. Customer loyalty in today's banking environment is frankly unstable. Sensory branding may be the banks' only route back to a human-centered environment.

The Retail Industry

Retail has made steady strides in sensory branding over the past decade. First, music was introduced in some stores, then environmental designers altered stores' layouts and décor, and today, they're making use of aromas. Problem is, apart from Abercrombie & Fitch, all this sensory progress is nonbranded. Very few chains are developing their own branded sound, tactile-designed bags, or packaging. But over the next couple of years we should see this trend reverse itself.

Technology will also push retailers in the right sensory direction. What's up next? Sonic branding: sonic logos incorporated into packaging that will play branded tunes when you open them. Nonbranded sonics are already hard at work: Just as the escalators in the Hong Kong airport inform you when it's time to step off, a voice will appear out of nowhere in your supermarket to let you know when the next checkout line is available.

The Fashion Industry

In 2002 Prada revolutionized dressing rooms in its Soho store in New York City by installing "smart" closets. Smart closets scan a customer's individual, electronic chip-based clothing tags and then send the garment information to an interactive touch screen in the cubicle. The customer can then use the screen to select other sizes, colors, or fabrics. The screen also displays video footage of the garment being worn on the Prada catwalk.

Retail and fashion have come together to create an entertainment experience, using technology that communicates via an increasing number of senses. Today, microchips are able to identify an "anticolor clash," which informs female (and even male) shoppers if a new piece of clothing matches their existing wardrobe. Once consumers commit to buying an item, a chip will politely inform them the best way to take care of it.

As far as sensory branding goes, the fashion industry is fast catching up to the perfume industry—which is a good thing.

The Entertainment Industry

Increasingly, more merchandising programs piggyback on the movies that show up at your local cineplex. More than one film has a corresponding ride in a theme park (think *Pirates of the Caribbean*). The entertainment industry is doing fantastically well in the sensory branding department. Will it last, though? On average, a film has a financial lifespan of six months. When the box office declines, the ride or game will lose its relevance, making it hard to justify a permanent Indiana Jones or Harry Potter ride in Disneyland or Warner Brothers World.

The sensory branding integration among movies, cinemas, merchandising, theme parks, and events is very often questionable. More than three thousand items of merchandise reside under the Harry Potter umbrella, and share little in common except that they're made in China and brandish the Harry Potter logo. Harry never invented his own smell. Neither was he characterized by a special sound, touch, or taste. Harry Potter merchandise appeals only to the eye. It has no sensory links to the movies, the rides, or even J. K. Rowling's seven magnificent books. Nope—Harry Potter gear is just more merchandising, which probably won't extend beyond the franchise's lifespan.

The Gaming Industry

Computer games are fearlessly venturing into a whole new sensory universe via technology. Many games seek to simulate the real world. Tetris, the ever-popular 3-D game, will soon be reformatted with surround sound and tactile stimulation. There are more than 100 million eager gamers out there, providing all the motivation inventors and technology companies need to import and convey as many sensory touch points as possible.

Over the next few years the computer gaming industry will push mass sensory communication even further by rolling out a variety of mice and joysticks to a world where roughly 30 percent of computer game aficionados are in front of their consoles several times a week.

Real tactile experiences are already a reality. The Immersion Corporation has released TouchWare Gaming, which the company promotes as a "Touch sense technology [which] can transform any game into a multi-sensory experience by engaging your sense of touch." TouchWare Gaming is already for sale to consumers. With it, you can "feel your light saber hum" and "your shotgun blast and reload." You'll also know if "your missile locks on a target" or if your car's "driving over cobblestones."[3]

With its stylish black paint job, the Nostromo n30 mouse looks like any other rollerball computer mouse. However what you see is *not* what you get, because this mouse is embedded with TouchWare technology. In sync with the visuals on the screen, the mouse whirs through a palette of vibrations, which make their way to your fingertips. Sony PlayStation's game controller offers a different type of feedback—known as "rumble"—which allows gamers to feel every bump, impact, and crash in whatever game they're playing. The SideWinder Force Feedback 2 joystick from Microsoft even supports force feedback—which is the sensation users experience in their hands as they play certain games.

Sensory Excellence

The World's Top Sensory Brands

Based on input from focus groups across the world, our Brand Sense study analyzed the world's top brands from a sensory excellence perspective. Among the two hundred most valuable brands according to Interbrand, it became clear that very few take advantage of their sensory potential. Fewer than 10 percent of these brands, in fact, demonstrate anything close to a sensory branding platform, although five years from now, this figure will be up to 35 percent.

We used the following criteria to assess the twenty most valuable brands:

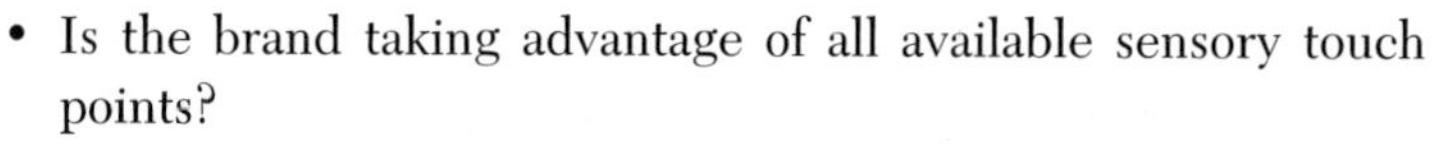

- Is the brand taking advantage of all available sensory touch points?
- Is there a strong, consistent connection across each of the touch points?
- To what degree does the brand reflect an innovative sensory mind-set that sets it apart from its competitors?
- To what extent do consumers associate these sensory signals with this particular brand—and how authentic do they perceive these signals to be?
- How distinct and integrated are these signals for the consumer?

The most intriguing revelation? The majority of the top twenty brands that take advantage of a multisensory platform have even more potential than what we've seen to date. Louis Vuitton's steady growth of merchandise gives it free rein to ensure a four-, if not five-sense appeal. Nokia's steady growth of digital channels represents even more sensory opportunities (including the company's icon, sound, and navigation features). Gillette needs to focus on their inconsistencies in tactile and aroma-based signals, and Starbucks still has a long way to go to capitalize on their sensory appeal in their many stores, where their own lines of merchandise tend to be neglected—and where it today is a fact that their customers, accord-

RANK	BRAND	SENSORY LEVERAGE (in percent)
1	Singapore Airlines	96.3
2	Apple	91.3
3	Disney	87.6
4	Mercedes-Benz	78.8
5	Marlboro	75.0
6	Tiffany	73.8
7	Louis Vuitton	72.5
8	Bang & Olufsen	71.3
9	Nokia	70.0
10	Harley-Davidson	68.8
11	Nike	67.5
12	Absolut Vodka	65.0
13	Coca-Cola	63.8
14	Gillette	62.5
15	Pepsi	61.3
16	Starbucks	60.0
17	Prada	58.8
18	Caterpillar	57.5
19	Guinness	56.3
20	Rolls-Royce	55.0

FIGURE 7.1 Top 20 sensory excellent brands. Which brands can today be considered the world's top sensory brands? An extensive evaluation of the world's 200 most valuable brands reveals the members of the exclusive club.

ing to the Brand Sense study, don't relate a distinct taste to Starbucks at all (other than that sour milk smell we talked about before).

But This Is Just the Very Beginning . . .

Even if you can tick every sensory box for the brands you love, claiming that every sensory aspect of your brand has been fulfilled—well, it's far from the end of your sensory story. From my perspective, there's every indication in the world that branding will move into

RANK	BRAND	SENSORY LEVERAGE (in percent)
1	Ikea	23.8
2	Motorola	25.0
3	Virgin	26.3
4	KFC	28.8
5	Adidas	31.3
6	Sony	31.3
7	Burger King	31.3
8	McDonald's	32.5
9	Kleenex	32.5
10	Microsoft	33.8
11	Philips	33.8
12	Barbie	33.8
13	Nescafé	35.0
14	Nintendo	36.3
15	Kodak	40.0
16	AOL	41.3
17	Wrigley	42.5
18	Colgate	43.8
19	IBM	45.0
20	Ford	46.3

FIGURE 7.2 Top 20 brands with the largest untapped sensory potential. A range of top brands has so far missed out on the sensory potential—this includes this list covering the brands representing the largest untapped sensory potential.

even more sophisticated realms, namely brands that not only anchor themselves in tradition, but also adopt religious characteristics and use sensory branding as a holistic way of spreading the news.

NASA named its first space shuttle The Enterprise, thanks to 400,000 or so requests from *Star Trek* fans all around the world. *Star Trek*, after all, was more than a television show. It evolved into an all-enveloping brand with a religious following, complete with its own language, characters, sounds, and design. Remember: very few brands have succeeded in turning customers into evangelists—and from Apple to Harley-Davidson to Prada, customers' lifelong belief in a product or company forms one of the most essential building blocks in creating a triumphant brand.

Highlights

Fewer than 10 percent of the world's top brands demonstrate a sensory branding platform, although within the next five years, this figure will jump to 35 percent, a development that will take place within the following three categories of industry:

1. **The sensory pioneers.** Over the next decade, the automobile and pharmaceutical industries will lead the way in sensory focus and innovation.
2. **The sensory adopters.** The telecommunications and computer industries are both fighting for definition and differentiation in their rivals. For inspiration, they're most likely to look to the automobile and entertainment sectors for inspiration.
3. **The sensory followers.** This, a broad collection of industries including retail, Fast-Moving-Consumer-Goods and entertainment, is more likely to trail than to lead.

The future of sensory brands will be evaluated on the following criteria:

- Is the brand taking advantage of all available sensory touch points?
- Is there a strong, consistent synergy across each of the touch points?
- To what degree does the brand reflect an innovative sensory mind-set that sets it apart from its competitors?
- To what extent does the consumer associate these sensory signals with this particular brand—and how authentic do they perceive these signals to be?
- How distinct and integrated are these signals for the consumer?

From what I can tell, there's every indication that branding will move into even more sophisticated realms that not only anchor themselves in tradition but also adopt religious characteristics and use sensory branding as a holistic way of spreading the news. After all, when you think about it, could there be anything more smashable?

Notes

2. Maybe I'm Doing It Right?

1. http://www.aap.org/advocacy/washing/Testimonies-Statements-Petitions/06-22-07-Media-and-Kids-Testimony.pdf.
2. TV Turnoff Network, www.tvturnoff.org.
3. http://af-za.facebook.com/notes.php?id=33849124322.
4. http://www.scentmarketing.org/doc/11Newsletter.pdf.
5. http://www.telegraph.co.uk/foodanddrink/foodanddrinknews/5884340/Adverts-work-best-when-appealing-to-all-senses.html.
6. http://www.emarketer.com/Article.aspx?R=1006813.
7. BRAND-DRIVEN Conference Report (2009) at http://www.creativenz.govt.nz/LinkClick.aspx?fileticket=%2BFCoWyFOZYg%3D&tabid=4895&language=en-NZ.
8. Nielsen Media Research.
9. http://brandchannel.com/features_effect.asp?pf_id=453.
10. http://www.commercialalert.org/issues/culture/ad-creep/whats-that-smell-in-the-movie-theater-its-an-ad.
11. H. A. Roth (1988), "Psychological relationships between perceived sweetness and color in lemon-and-lime flavored drinks," *Journal of Food Science*, 53:1116–1119.
12. C. N. DuBose (1980), "Effects of colorants and flavorants on identification, perceived flavor intensity, and hedonic quality of fruit-flavored beverages and cake," *Journal of Food Science*, 45:1393–1399, 1415.
13. Quoted in Ackerman, p. 191.
14. http://www.brandinfection.com/2006/02/07/dogs-love-pedigree/
15. Diane Ackerman (1990), *A natural history of the senses*, Vintage Books, New York, p. 191.
16. Lyall Watson (2000), *Jacobson's organ: and the remarkable nature of smell*, W. W. Norton & Company, New York, p. 7.
17. Ibid. p. 88.
18. Ibid. p. 90.

19. Ibid. p. 136.
20. Boyd Gibbons (1986), "The intimate sense of smell," *National Geographic*, September, p. 324.
21. Ashley Montagu (1986), *Touching: the human significance of the skin*, Harper & Row, New York, 3rd ed., p. 238.

3. A Smash Hit

1. http://www/ftc.gov/os/2007/06/cabebw.pdf.
2. Brand Sense study, 2003.
3. www.benetton.com.
4. www.quickstart.clari.net/qs_se/webnews/wed/bz/Bpa-heinz.RaYS_DSA.html.
5. http://www.brandonbournonbeerclub.com/milky-russian-vodka-in-a-breast-shaped-bottle.html.
6. www.press.nokia.com/PR/199810/778408_5.html.
7. Ibid.
8. www.absolut.com.
9. www.fredericksburg.com/News/FLS/2002/102002/10032002/747192.

4. And Then There Were Five

1. Discovery Communications Inc., 2000.
2. BRANDchild study carried out by Millward Brown, 2002.
3. Ronald E. Millman (1985), "The influence of background music on the behaviour of restaurant patrons," *Journal of Consumer Research,* vol. 13.
4. Judy I. Alpert and Mark I. Alpert (1988), "Background music as an influence in consumer mood and advertising responses," in Thomas K. Scrull (ed.), *Advances in Consumer Research,* 16, pp. 485–91.
5. Kevin Ferguson, "Coin-free slot jackpots? Unclinkable!" at http://www.reviewjournal.com/lvrj_home/2000/Aug-28-Mon-2000/business/14239785.html.
6. http://news.moneycentral.msn.com/ticker/article.aspx?symbol=US:HOT&feed=BW&date=20090924&id=10421787.
7. http://www.walletpop.com/blog/2009/07/27/nissan-knows-youre-sleepy-sends-a-scent-to-keep-you-alert/.
8. Richard E. Peck (2001), "Bill Gates bite of the Big Apple," at www.ltn-archive.hotresponse.com/december01/.
9. Diane M. Szaflarski, "How we see: The first steps of human vision" at www.accessexcellence.org/AE/AEC/CC/vision_background.html.
10. Sarah Ellison and Erin White (2000), "Sensory marketeers say the way to reach shoppers is by the nose," *Financial Express,* 27 November.
11. www.hersheypa.com/index.html.

12. Ken Leach, *Perfume Presentation: 100 Years of Artistry,* quoted on www.wpbs.com.
13. Warren and Warrenburg (1993), "Effects of Smell on Emotions," *Journal of Experimental Psychology,* 113 (4): 394–409.
14. Amanda Gardner (2003), "Odors Conjure Up Awful 9/11 Memories," at www.healthfinder.gov/news/newsstory.asp?docID=513682.
15. http://www.luxematic.com/?p=1081.
16. http://eab.sagepub.com/egi/content/abstract/41/2/258.
17. http://www.neurosciencemarketing.com/blog/articles/sensory-branding-at-le-meridien.htm.
18. http://www.scentmarketing.org/doc/8newsletter.pdf.
19. http://online.wsj.com/article/SB124277733367437141.html.
20. Christopher Koch and Eric C. Koch (2003), "Preconceptions of taste based on color," *Journal of Psychology*, May, pp. 233–42.
21. Trygg Engen, "Benefits of fragrances," Olfactory Research Funds, New York, p. 5.
22. J. Stephan Jellinek (2003), "The underestimated power of implicit fragrance research," and Pieter Aarts, "Fragrances with real impact," papers presented at Fragrance Research Conference, Lausanne, 16–18 March.
23. www.theecologist.org/archive_article.html?article=342&category=33.

6. Moving Mountains

1. http://www.marketresearch.com/product/display.asp?productid=1692979&SID=36686314-456007258-419551152&kw=Religious.
2. http://www.perceptnet.com/cient04_08_ang.htm.
3. http://www.publishers.org/main/IndustryStats/documents/S12007Final.pdf.
4. http://www.isn.ne.jp/~suzutayu/Kitty/KittyPray-e.html.
5. Matthew W. Ragas and Bolivar J. Bueno (2002), *The power of cult branding: How 9 magnetic brands turned customers into loyal followers (and yours can too!),* Prima Venture, New York, p. 28.
6. Sean Dodson (2002), "The world within," *Sydney Morning Herald,* Icon, May 23.

7. The Future

1. Alfred Hermida (2003), "Mobiles get a sense of touch," at www.news.bbc.co.uk/1/hi/technology/2677813.stm, January 21.
2. www.vtplayer.free.fr.
3. Immersion Corporation, "Feel the game with TouchWare gaming," at www.immersion.com/gaming.

The Brand Sense Research

In 2003, Martin Lindstrom approached Millward Brown, a leading and innovating global market research agency specializing in helping companies maximize their brand equity and brand performance. He had an unusual request: "Help me prove that the sensory experience of brands plays a key role in creating brand loyalty." While our clients around the world have approached us with many questions related to the effectiveness of their brand-building and marketing activities, this one was unique. After all, we experience the world through our senses, so intuitively it seemed obvious that brands could create a stronger emotional bond by taking advantage of their sensory appeal. The question was, was there any way to prove it?

To do so we designed a two-stage research program that spanned the globe, involving hundreds of researchers and interviewing thousands of people.

Stage One: Understanding the Role of the Senses

When tackling a new and unique project like this, it is crucial to understand the mental "landscape" in which brands exist. Qualitative research, where a trained moderator explores ideas and brand associations using projective techniques with small groups of people, is invaluable, providing insights and guiding the way to a more quantitative measurement.

We conducted focus groups in thirteen countries: Chile, Denmark, Holland, India, Japan, Mexico, Poland, Spain, South Africa, Sweden, Thailand, the United Kingdom, and the United States. In each country we spoke with males and females from the ages of twenty-five to forty. Our exploration focused on ten global brands: Coke, Mercedes-Benz,

Dove, Ford, Gillette, Vodafone/Disney, Levi's, Sony, Nike, and McDonald's. Five additional local brands (which varied by market) were also included in the mix.

Our findings gave us a good understanding of the role of the senses in creating brand loyalty, and confirmed that brands with sensory depth were particularly strong, with clearly defined, globally understood, and distinctive brand identities, not to mention relevant and aspirational brand values. In some respects, these brands had deliberately built their sensory values, and were now benefiting from these associations.

Stage Two: Quantifying the Influence of the Senses

In many ways this was the most challenging phase of the research. We now wanted to prove that the memory of a brand's sensory associations increased a consumer's desire to buy the brand.

To do so, we created and tested a unique online questionnaire. In conjunction with our partner, Lightspeed Online Research, we interviewed over two thousand people in the United States, the UK, and Japan, who provided feedback on their sensory associations, imagery, purchase intent, and much more, for eighteen brands.

We then used a statistical methodology called structural equation modeling to test hypotheses (from stage one) on how the senses might affect brand loyalty. Several models based on the varying hypotheses of how the variables interrelate were developed for the same set of data. Each model was then evaluated by a combination of diagnostics associated with its individual paths as well as an overall goodness-of-fit index. The model with the best overall fit and intuitively sensible paths was chosen as the best representation of reality.

Robert D. Meyers
Group CEO, Millward Brown

A Few Words from the Researcher

We all know the trends. Number of brands up. Price competition up. Media options up. The barriers to marketing success are becoming ever higher. Marketers today face a tough job trying to keep their brands healthy and profitable. Millward Brown's mission is to help them do so by providing insights into how to build and maintain brands in this increasingly complex world, which is why we were eager to develop the research findings for this book.

Today's complex marketing world requires us to understand the impact of all the different influences on a purchase decision.

Take the case of digital cameras. Job number one is to make sure that your brand is considered when people first start thinking about buying one. That means sowing the seeds early, through traditional advertising, viral marketing, and publicity. No one, however, buys a camera without checking the price. Send the wrong signals and a brand can easily get ruled out simply because people think it's too expensive.

Good job—you are now on the shopping list! Now it is down to features and price, right? Wrong! Very few brands get rejected on the grounds of performance or price. Almost every brand of camera offers a wide range of features and prices so that most people can find *something* that meets their needs and budgets. What, then, determines the purchase decision? For many it is how the camera looks, feels, and sounds. Does it feel good to use? Does it look cool or purposeful? Does it make the right noises? Based on their experience of using film cameras, people expect to hear a click and a whir when taking a photograph. Not hearing that sound made people uncomfortable with some of the early digital cameras. The latest digitals use sounds reminiscent of film cameras to signal that yes, a photograph has been taken. Often the smallest things can swing a purchase decision.

The very absence of anything other than a visual experience prevents many consumers from buying online. Even the most aggressive proponents of Internet shopping limit the potential size of the market because sensory perception is crucial. In the case of digital cameras, only one in four recent purchasers in the United States claims to have bought his or her camera online. In the case of automotive brands, consumers use the Internet to research facts, options, and prices, but practically all of them visit a showroom before making a final decision. It's the responsiveness of the ear to the controls, the seat comfort, even the smell, that seal the deal. Buying a new car is both a serious decision and a sensuous experience. To buy a car based on sight alone would leave most people dissatisfied, not to mention worried that they'd somehow made a mistake. Regardless of the product or service, most people will always want to experience touch, smell, sound, and taste, as well as visual appeal, before they buy.

In the modern day and age marketers have largely neglected the power of the senses, favoring instead the cool rationality of product specifications and the cut and thrust of price discounts. That is another reason why the senses offer a potent means of communication, helping marketers to find new ways to differentiate their brands and strike an emotional chord in consumers. After all, our senses are such a fundamental part of being human that they are inescapable! They influence us every second of the day. Marketers who recognize the power of the senses will find a new means of building long-lasting bonds with their consumers. No—not one based on discounts and loyalty programs, but one based on enjoyment and appreciation.

Martin Lindstrom has explored the sensory arena with the same enthusiasm that he has displayed when tackling the Internet or the lives of today's tweens. Our research was designed to help him illustrate the impact of the senses and to demonstrate how the senses impact brand choice and loyalty. I believe the combination has made this book a great read which will help you see the branding world with new eyes.

Nigel Hollis

Acknowledgments

I am indebted to Nigel Hollis, the global strategic planning director for Millward Brown. He has extensive experience in market research, and his particular expertise includes advertising pre-testing, brand equity research, online research, and how marketing communications can build and maintain brands. His career at Millward Brown has spanned the Atlantic; he has worked for major Fortune 500 clients, covering packaged goods, automotive, alcoholic beverages, financial services, IT, and travel categories.

It would be impossible to mention everyone who contributed to the ideas and knowledge I've drawn on for this book. Close to six hundred researchers have assimilated data, provided insight, and worked hard to make Brand Sense a truly global project.

First and foremost, Peter Smith and Lynne Segal. It's the third book we've worked on together. In short, if they quit editing, I'd quit writing. Also a sincere thanks to my superb agent James Levine, and the impressive team at Free Press: Suzanne Donahue, Carisa Hays, and Michele Jacob.

Once again the Millward Brown organization has been a pleasure to work with. Without their support for this global project, it would have been almost impossible to execute. They have verified my assumptions, and taken the research where no other marketer has gone before—into a tactile world full of smells and tastes. Again, a sincere thanks to Nigel Hollis (U.S.). He managed the research project with skill, professionalism, and perpetual optimism. Thanks to Eileen Campbell (U.S.) and Andrea Bielli (Italy) who have given enormous support behind the scenes, Andreas Grotholt (Germany) for his ongoing feedback, and

Andreas Gonzales (Australia) for his generosity from the very first day I knocked at his door.

Several people around the world have helped me capture the essense of sensory branding. These include Karen Elstein (UK), Andres Lopez, and Claudia Jauregui (Mexico), Mauricio Yuraszeck, Marco Zunino, and Maria Cristina Moya (Chile), Chaniya Nakalugshana and Tanes Chalermvongsavej (Thailand), Asif Noorani (Japan), Das Sharmila, Ghai Harjyoti, and Neerja Wable (India), Christine Malone and Kim South Hyde (South Africa), Pawel Ciacek (Poland), Andrei Ackles (Canada), Toni Parra (Spain), Inge Cootjans, Astrid DeJong, and Megumi Ishida (Netherlands), Lars Andersen and Julie Hoffmann Jeppesen (Denmark), and Ola Mobolade, Janette Ponticello, Bill Brannon, Dave Hluska, Doreen Harmon, Wes Covalt, Ariana Marra, Brian LoCicero, Brian Gilgren, Dusty Byrd, Mark Karambelas, Heather Fitzgerald, and Christina Swatton, all from the United States. I would also like to thank Lightspeed Online Research in the USA and have not forgotten Knots sample provider in Japan.

Since writing *BRANDchild* and *Buyology*, I've had the good fortune to meet inspiring people across the globe who have inspired me and helped to make this book more challenging and stimulating. Finally, I remain indebted to the many readers who sent me their amazing feedback, and the thousands of people all over the world who answered endless questionnaires and patiently discussed the five senses in the many focus groups. Branding is about feelings, and their feelings—and now, I hope yours—have been an essential contribution to this book.

Index

Index

Index

Index

Index

About the Author

Martin Lindstrom is the *New York Times* and *Wall Street Journal* best-selling author of *Buyology: Truth and Lies About Why We Buy* (Doubleday). He is the CEO and chairman of the Lindstrom Company and the chairman of Buyology, Inc. (New York) and Brand Sense Agency (London).

As one of the world's 100 most influential people according to *Time* magazine, Lindstrom advises top executives at companies including the McDonald's Corporation, Nestlé, Procter & Gamble, Microsoft Corporation, The Walt Disney Company, Pepsi, Unilever, and GlaxoSmith-Kline. Lindstrom speaks to a global audience of close to a million people every year. He has been featured in numerous publications, including *Wall Street Journal, New York Times, Washington Post, USA Today, Forbes, Fortune, Newsweek, BusinessWeek, People Magazine, Wallpaper, Harvard Business Review, The Times, The Guardian, New York Post, Chicago Tribune, The Economist,* and *Time*. He has also been featured on NBC's *Today* show, ABC News, CNN, CBS, Discovery, FOX, and the BBC. *Brand Sense* was acclaimed by the *Wall Street Journal* as one of the five best marketing books ever published.

Buyology was voted business book of the year by *USA Today* and reached all ten of the top bestseller lists in the United States and worldwide during 2008 and 2009. His five books on branding have been translated into thirty-seven languages and published in more than eighty countries. Lindstrom is a frequent contributor to the *New York Times, Parade,* and *Advertising Age* and is a regular contributor to NBC's *Today* show with his ongoing series "Marketing Mind Games."

Kogan Page